Comfort Cooking

Heartwarming Recipes for Cozy Meals

Milton Powers

loss due to the information herein, either directly or indirectly. Respective authors own all copyrights not held by the publisher. The information herein is offered for informational purposes solely, and is universal as so. The presentation of the information is without contract or any type of guarantee assurance. The trademarks that are used are without any consent, and the publication of the trademark is without permission or backing by the trademark owner. All trademarks and brands within this book are for clarifying purposes only and are the owned by the owners themselves, not affiliated with this document.

Table of Contents

Chapter 1

Introduction

What is Comfort Cooking?

Comfort cooking embodies more than just the act of preparing meals; it's about creating experiences that nourish both the body and soul. At its core, comfort cooking is deeply personal, often rooted in tradition and memory, evoking feelings of warmth, love, and safety. It's the kind of cooking that brings people together, fostering a sense of community and belonging, even if it's just for a fleeting moment around the dinner table.

The essence of comfort cooking lies in its ability to provide solace and joy. Whether it's a steaming bowl of chicken noodle soup on a cold day or a plate of warm cookies fresh from the oven, these dishes have a unique way of making us feel at home. They are often simple, hearty, and full of flavor, designed to be enjoyed slowly and savored. The process of making these meals can be just as comforting as eating them. The rhythmic chopping of vegetables, the aromatic simmering of broth, and the gentle kneading of dough all contribute to a therapeutic experience that can help soothe the mind and spirit.

One of the hallmarks of comfort cooking is its emphasis on familiar ingredients and time-tested recipes. These dishes don't require exotic or expensive ingredients; instead, they rely on pantry staples and seasonal produce. Think of the rich, creamy texture of mashed potatoes, the satisfying crunch of a well-baked pie crust, or the tender juiciness of a roasted chicken. These are the flavors and textures that many of us grew up with, and they carry with them a sense of nostalgia and warmth.

Comfort cooking also highlights the importance of balance and moderation. It's about enjoying rich, indulgent foods without guilt, but also recognizing the value of wholesome, nourishing ingredients. A perfect example is a hearty beef stew, which combines tender chunks of meat with an abundance of root vegetables, all slowly cooked to perfection. This dish is not only delicious but also packed with nutrients, making it a satisfying and balanced meal.

Another key aspect of comfort cooking is its adaptability. While there are classic comfort foods that many of us are familiar with, such as mac and cheese or chicken pot pie, the concept of comfort food can vary greatly from person to person and culture to culture. For some, it might be a spicy curry that brings back memories of family gatherings, while for others, it might be a simple bowl of rice and beans that reminds them of home. The beauty of comfort cooking is that it can be tailored to individual tastes and preferences, making it a deeply personal and meaningful practice.

The process of comfort cooking often involves slow cooking methods that allow flavors to meld and deepen over time. Techniques such as braising, roasting, and simmering are commonly used, as they tend to enhance the natural flavors of the ingredients and create rich, complex dishes. These methods also encourage a slower pace in the kitchen, allowing the cook to engage fully with the process and enjoy the sensory experiences of cooking.

In addition to the sensory pleasures, comfort cooking also has emotional and psychological benefits. The act of preparing a meal for oneself or others can be a powerful way to express love and care. Sharing a home-cooked meal can strengthen bonds and create lasting memories. There's something profoundly comforting about knowing that someone has taken the time and effort to prepare a meal with you in mind.

Comfort cooking is also about resilience and resourcefulness. It often involves making the most of what you have on hand, whether it's using up leftover ingredients or transforming simple staples into something special. This approach not only reduces waste but also encourages creativity and innovation in the kitchen. A pot of vegetable soup, for example, can be made from a variety of odds and ends from the fridge, resulting in a delicious and satisfying meal that is greater than the sum of its parts.

The rituals and routines associated with comfort cooking can provide a sense of stability and predictability in an often chaotic world. The familiar steps of preparing a favorite dish can be grounding and reassuring, offering a sense of control and accomplishment. For many, the kitchen becomes a sanctuary, a place where they can find solace and peace amidst the busyness of everyday life.

Comfort cooking is not just about the food itself, but also about the experiences and memories associated with it. Many of us have fond recollections of cooking alongside a parent or grandparent, learning cherished family recipes, and sharing stories and laughter over a meal. These moments are often imbued with a sense of warmth and love that transcends the food on the plate.

In today's fast-paced world, comfort cooking can serve as a reminder to slow down and savor the simple pleasures of life. It encourages us to be present in the moment and to appreciate the sensory and emotional experiences of cooking and eating. Whether it's the feel of dough beneath your hands, the aroma of onions sautéing in butter, or the first bite of a perfectly baked cookie, these small moments of joy can have a profound impact on our overall well-being.

Ultimately, comfort cooking is about creating a sense of home, no matter where you are. It's about finding joy in the process of cooking and sharing that joy with others. Whether you're cooking for yourself, your family, or your friends, the act of preparing and sharing a meal is a powerful way to connect and nurture both body and soul.

The Importance of Cozy Meals

The importance of cozy meals cannot be overstated. They serve as an anchor in our daily lives, providing comfort, nourishment, and a sense of connection. These meals are more than just sustenance; they are an expression of care, a way to celebrate the simple joys of life, and an opportunity to create lasting memories with loved ones.

Cozy meals have a unique ability to evoke feelings of warmth and safety. Think about the comforting aroma of a pot roast slowly cooking in the oven, or the satisfaction of dipping a piece of crusty bread into a bowl of hearty soup on a chilly evening. These sensory experiences are deeply rooted in our memories and emotions, often reminding us of home, family, and cherished traditions. The act of preparing and sharing a cozy meal can transform an ordinary day into something special, creating a sense of occasion even in the midst of routine.

One of the key aspects of cozy meals is their power to bring people together. In a world where our lives are increasingly busy and fragmented, sitting down to a shared meal can be a rare and precious opportunity to connect with others. Whether it's a family dinner, a gathering of friends, or a quiet evening with a loved one, the act of sharing food fosters a sense of community and belonging. Conversations flow more easily around the dinner table, creating an environment where stories are told, laughter is shared, and bonds are strengthened.

The importance of cozy meals is also evident in their ability to provide physical nourishment. These meals are often rich in nutrients, designed to be satisfying and wholesome. A well-balanced cozy meal typically includes a variety of food groups, ensuring that we receive the vitamins, minerals, and energy we need to thrive. For example, a classic beef stew with tender chunks of meat, a medley of root vegetables, and a flavorful broth provides protein, fiber, and essential nutrients in every bite. Similarly, a pasta bake with a mix of vegetables, lean protein, and whole grains offers a balanced and hearty dish that can sustain us through the day.

In addition to their nutritional value, cozy meals often emphasize the use of fresh, seasonal ingredients. This not only enhances the flavor and quality of the dishes but also supports local farmers and promotes sustainable eating practices. By choosing ingredients that are in season, we can enjoy the natural bounty of each time of year, from the vibrant greens of spring to the hearty squashes of autumn. This connection to the seasons adds another layer of meaning to our meals, reminding us of the rhythms of nature and the importance of mindful eating.

The preparation of cozy meals can be a therapeutic and fulfilling activity in itself. The process of cooking allows us to slow down, focus on the present moment, and engage our senses. Chopping vegetables, stirring a simmering pot, or kneading dough can be meditative actions that help to reduce stress and promote a sense of calm. Cooking also provides an opportunity for creativity and self-expression, as we experiment with flavors, textures, and techniques to create dishes that bring us joy.

For beginners, the idea of preparing cozy meals might seem daunting, but it doesn't have to be. The beauty of cozy cooking lies in its simplicity and accessibility. Many beloved cozy dishes are straightforward to prepare, requiring only basic ingredients and techniques. For instance, a classic chicken noodle soup can be made with just a few staple ingredients: chicken, noodles, carrots, celery, and broth. The key is to focus on the quality of the ingredients and the care you put into the preparation, rather than striving for perfection or complexity.

Cozy meals also play a significant role in self-care. Taking the time to prepare and enjoy a nourishing meal can be a powerful act of kindness towards oneself. In a fast-paced world where convenience often trumps quality, prioritizing homemade, wholesome food is a way to honor our bodies and well-being. It's a reminder that we deserve to eat well and take pleasure in our food, even amidst the demands of daily life.

Moreover, cozy meals can be a source of comfort during challenging times. Whether we're dealing with stress, illness, or emotional upheaval, a familiar and comforting dish can provide a sense of stability and reassurance. The ritual of cooking and eating can create a moment of respite, offering a small but significant way to care for ourselves and others. For instance, a bowl of creamy tomato basil soup on a rainy day can feel like a warm hug, providing both physical nourishment and emotional solace.

The importance of cozy meals extends to the cultural and historical significance they carry. Many traditional comfort foods have been passed down through generations, carrying with them the stories and heritage of our ancestors. These dishes often reflect the values, resources, and ingenuity of the communities that created them. By preparing and sharing these foods, we not only preserve our culinary heritage but also deepen our connection to our roots and history.

In a multicultural society, cozy meals also provide an opportunity to explore and appreciate the diverse culinary traditions around us. Trying out recipes from different cultures can broaden our palates and deepen our understanding of the world. It's a way to celebrate diversity and foster a sense of curiosity and openness. For example, preparing a fragrant curry or a savory dumpling soup can transport us to another part of the world, bringing a sense of adventure and discovery to our dining table.

Ultimately, the importance of cozy meals lies in their ability to nourish us on multiple levels. They provide physical sustenance, emotional comfort, and a sense of connection to others and to ourselves. They remind us of the joys of simple, wholesome food and the power of shared experiences. In a world that often values speed and efficiency over quality and care, cozy meals offer a counterbalance, inviting us to slow down, savor the moment, and find joy in the act of cooking and eating.

Ingredients that Warm the Soul

Imagine returning home on a blustery winter evening, cheeks flushed from the cold, and being greeted by the rich, savory scent of a stew simmering on the stove. The warmth envelops you as you step inside, the promise of a hearty meal inviting you to relax and unwind. Ingredients that warm the soul are those that transform simple dishes into comforting experiences, leaving us feeling nourished and loved.

One of the most profound ingredients that warms the soul is a good broth or stock. Whether it's chicken, beef, vegetable, or bone broth, this foundational liquid forms the base of countless comforting dishes. The process of making broth itself is an act of patience and care. Slowly simmering bones, vegetables, and herbs extracts deep, rich flavors and nutrients, resulting in a liquid that is both nourishing and versatile. A well-made broth can serve as the base for soups, stews, risottos, and even gravies, infusing each dish with a layer of warmth and complexity.

Root vegetables are another essential ingredient for soul-warming meals. Potatoes, carrots, parsnips, and sweet potatoes not only offer a hearty texture but also bring a natural sweetness and earthiness to dishes. Roasting these vegetables enhances their flavors, caramelizing their sugars and creating a satisfying contrast between their crispy exteriors and tender interiors. A simple tray of roasted root vegetables, seasoned with olive oil, salt, and herbs, can be a comforting side dish or a substantial addition to salads and grain bowls.

Beans and legumes also play a crucial role in creating dishes that warm the soul. Their ability to absorb flavors and add body to soups, stews, and casseroles makes them invaluable in comfort cooking. Lentils, chickpeas, black beans, and cannellini beans are just a few examples of the wide variety available. These ingredients are not only filling and nutritious but also versatile. A pot of lentil soup, seasoned with garlic, onions, and a touch of cumin, can be both hearty and heartwarming. Similarly, a chickpea curry with tomatoes, coconut milk, and warming spices like turmeric and ginger can provide a comforting and satisfying meal.

Speaking of spices, they are indispensable in the realm of soul-warming ingredients. Spices like cinnamon, nutmeg, cloves, and allspice evoke a sense of warmth and comfort, especially in baked goods and sweet dishes. A sprinkle of cinnamon can transform a simple bowl of oatmeal into a cozy breakfast treat, while nutmeg adds depth to creamy sauces and casseroles. For savory dishes, spices like cumin, coriander, and smoked paprika bring warmth and complexity, enhancing the flavors of roasted meats, stews, and vegetable dishes.

Herbs also contribute significantly to the comforting nature of a meal. Fresh herbs like rosemary, thyme, sage, and parsley not only add vibrant flavors but also bring a sense of freshness and vitality to dishes. A sprig of rosemary can elevate a roasted chicken, while thyme and sage can add depth to stuffing or a pot of beans. Freshly chopped parsley sprinkled over a finished dish can brighten the flavors and add a touch of color, making the meal feel more inviting and complete.

Grains and pasta are classic comfort food ingredients that warm the soul through their hearty and satisfying nature. A steaming bowl of risotto, made with Arborio rice slowly cooked in broth and finished with Parmesan cheese, is the epitome of comfort. Similarly, a plate of pasta tossed in a rich, meaty Bolognese sauce or a creamy Alfredo sauce can provide a sense of indulgence and contentment. Whole grains like quinoa, farro, and barley also bring a satisfying chewiness and nutty flavor to soups and salads, making them hearty and nourishing.

Cheese, with its rich and creamy texture, is another ingredient that has the power to warm the soul. Whether it's melted into a gooey mac and cheese, sprinkled over a bubbling lasagna, or crumbled on top of a hearty winter salad, cheese adds a comforting richness that is hard to resist. The variety of cheeses available, from sharp Cheddar to creamy

Brie to tangy blue cheese, allows for endless possibilities in creating comforting and soul-warming dishes.

Another ingredient that cannot be overlooked is bread. Freshly baked bread, with its crispy crust and soft, pillowy interior, is a universal symbol of comfort. The act of baking bread itself is a therapeutic and rewarding experience, filling the home with its irresistible aroma. A warm slice of bread, slathered with butter or dipped into a bowl of soup, can provide a simple yet profound sense of satisfaction and contentment.

Of course, we cannot discuss ingredients that warm the soul without mentioning chocolate. Whether it's a rich, dark chocolate bar, a mug of velvety hot cocoa, or a decadent chocolate cake, this beloved ingredient has a unique ability to provide comfort and joy. The deep, complex flavors of chocolate can evoke feelings of nostalgia and indulgence, making it a perfect ingredient for creating soul-warming desserts and treats.

Eggs, often overlooked, are another versatile and comforting ingredient. They can be the star of a simple yet satisfying meal, like a fluffy omelet filled with cheese and herbs, or a comforting bowl of ramen topped with a soft-boiled egg. Eggs also play a crucial role in baking, providing structure and richness to cakes, cookies, and custards. Their ability to transform into a multitude of comforting dishes makes them indispensable in the kitchen.

The importance of these soul-warming ingredients goes beyond their individual flavors and textures. They bring a sense of tradition and heritage, connecting us to our cultural roots and family histories. Many of these ingredients are staples in traditional comfort foods passed down through generations, carrying with them stories and memories. Preparing and enjoying these foods can be a way to honor and preserve these traditions, creating a sense of continuity and belonging.

Incorporating these ingredients into our cooking also encourages us to slow down and savor the process. The act of chopping vegetables, simmering a pot of broth, or kneading dough can be meditative and grounding, providing a respite from the busyness of daily life. Cooking with intention and care allows us to create meals that are not only nourishing but also deeply satisfying and comforting.

Moreover, using these ingredients can inspire creativity and exploration in the kitchen. Trying out new recipes and experimenting with different flavor combinations can be a fun and rewarding experience. It can also be a way to connect with others, whether it's cooking together with family and friends or sharing a homemade meal with loved ones. The joy and satisfaction that come from creating and sharing a soul-warming meal can be a powerful way to foster connection and build relationships.

Essential Kitchen Tools for Comfort Cooking

The heart of any kitchen is its tools, and when it comes to comfort cooking, having the right equipment can make all the difference. Essential kitchen tools not only streamline the cooking process but also enhance the flavors and textures of the dishes we cherish. These tools are the unsung heroes that transform simple ingredients into meals that evoke warmth and nostalgia.

A good chef's knife is the cornerstone of any kitchen. This versatile tool is indispensable for chopping vegetables, slicing meat, and dicing herbs. A high-quality chef's knife should feel balanced in your hand, with a sharp blade that glides effortlessly through food. Investing in a good knife and keeping it well-maintained with regular sharpening will make all your cooking tasks easier and more enjoyable.

Equally important is a sturdy cutting board. Wooden cutting boards are often preferred for their durability and gentle impact on knife blades. They provide a stable surface for slicing and dicing, and their natural wood grain can be kinder to your knives compared to plastic or glass. A large cutting board with ample space allows you to work more efficiently, keeping ingredients organized and preventing cross-contamination.

For many comfort dishes, a Dutch oven is a must-have. This heavy-duty pot, typically made of cast iron, is perfect for slow-cooking, braising, and making hearty stews and soups. Its thick walls and tight-fitting lid retain heat and moisture, ensuring that flavors meld beautifully over long cooking periods. Whether you're simmering a rich beef stew or baking a loaf of crusty bread, a Dutch oven is a versatile tool that delivers consistent, delicious results.

A set of reliable measuring cups and spoons is crucial for achieving the right balance of flavors in your recipes. Precision is key in both baking and cooking, and having accurate measurements ensures that your dishes turn out as intended. Stainless steel measuring cups and spoons are durable and easy to clean, making them a practical choice for any kitchen.

Mixing bowls in various sizes are essential for preparing and combining ingredients. Stainless steel or glass bowls are versatile and can be used for everything from marinating meat to mixing batter. Having a range of sizes allows you to choose the perfect bowl for the task at hand, whether you're whisking eggs for an omelet or tossing a salad.

A good set of cookware, including pots and pans, is the backbone of any kitchen. Nonstick skillets are excellent for cooking delicate items like eggs and pancakes, while stainless steel pans are ideal for searing meat and deglazing sauces. A heavy-bottomed saucepan is perfect for making creamy risottos and comforting soups. Investing in high-quality cookware ensures even heat distribution and durability, making your cooking experience smoother and more enjoyable.

For those who love baking, a stand mixer is a game-changer. This powerful appliance takes the labor out of mixing dough, whipping cream, and beating egg whites. With various attachments, a stand mixer can also handle tasks like kneading bread dough and grinding meat. Its consistent mixing results in perfectly textured doughs and batters, elevating your baking to new heights.

A slow cooker is another valuable tool for comfort cooking. It allows you to prepare meals with minimal effort, slowly cooking ingredients over several hours to develop deep, rich flavors. Whether you're making a hearty chili, a tender pot roast, or a creamy chicken soup, a slow cooker simplifies the process and ensures consistently delicious results.

An immersion blender, or stick blender, is a handy tool for pureeing soups, sauces, and even smoothies directly in the pot. This eliminates the need to transfer hot liquids to a traditional blender, reducing the risk of spills and burns. Its compact size makes it easy to store, and its versatility makes it a valuable addition to any kitchen.

For those who enjoy roasting, a reliable roasting pan is essential. A sturdy pan with a rack allows for even cooking and browning of meats and vegetables. The rack elevates the food, allowing heat to circulate and fat to drip away, resulting in perfectly roasted dishes. Whether you're preparing a holiday turkey or a simple weeknight roast chicken, a quality roasting pan ensures excellent results.

A digital thermometer is a small but mighty tool that takes the guesswork out of cooking meat. Ensuring that meat is cooked to the correct temperature is crucial for both safety and flavor. A digital thermometer provides an accurate reading in seconds, helping you achieve perfectly cooked roasts, steaks, and poultry every time.

In addition to these major tools, having a collection of smaller gadgets can also enhance your comfort cooking experience. A garlic press simplifies the process of mincing garlic, while a microplane grater is perfect for zesting citrus and grating hard cheeses.

A pair of kitchen shears can be used for a variety of tasks, from snipping herbs to cutting poultry.

A well-stocked pantry is another key element in comfort cooking. Keeping staples like flour, sugar, rice, pasta, and canned goods on hand ensures that you're always prepared to whip up a comforting meal. Spices and herbs, both fresh and dried, add depth and complexity to your dishes, turning simple recipes into flavorful feasts.

Organizing your kitchen tools and ingredients can make a significant difference in your cooking efficiency. Keeping frequently used tools within easy reach and storing ingredients in clear, labeled containers can streamline your workflow and reduce stress. A tidy kitchen not only looks inviting but also makes cooking more enjoyable.

Comfort cooking is as much about the process as it is about the final dish. Taking the time to prepare meals with care and intention can be a deeply satisfying experience. The right tools not only make this process easier but also inspire creativity and confidence in the kitchen. Whether you're an experienced cook or a beginner, having the essentials at your fingertips allows you to focus on what truly matters: creating delicious, heartwarming meals that bring joy and comfort to those who share them.

Chapter 2

Breakfast Bliss

Classic Pancakes and Variations

Few things evoke the comfort of home like a stack of classic pancakes, golden brown and drizzled with maple syrup. Pancakes are a versatile and beloved breakfast option that can be enjoyed plain or dressed up with a variety of toppings and mix-ins. This chapter delves into the art of making classic pancakes and explores a range of delightful variations to suit every palate.

To begin, it's essential to master the basic pancake recipe. The foundation of a good pancake lies in the balance of ingredients and the technique used to combine them. Start with the dry ingredients: one and a half cups of all-purpose flour, two tablespoons of granulated sugar, one tablespoon of baking powder, and half a teaspoon of salt. Whisk these together in a large bowl to ensure they are evenly distributed.

In a separate bowl, mix the wet ingredients: one and a quarter cups of milk, one large egg, and three tablespoons of melted butter. It's important that the milk is at room temperature and the melted butter is slightly cooled to prevent the egg from cooking prematurely. Combine these ingredients until they are fully incorporated.

The key to tender pancakes is in the mixing. Pour the wet ingredients into the dry ingredients and gently stir with a spatula until just combined. The batter should be slightly lumpy – over-mixing can result in tough, dense pancakes. Let the batter rest for five to ten minutes to allow the baking powder to activate and create a fluffier texture.

Preheat a non-stick skillet or griddle over medium heat. Lightly grease the surface with a small amount of butter or oil. Using a quarter-cup measure, pour the batter onto the skillet, spacing the pancakes a few inches apart. Cook until bubbles form on the surface and the edges look set, about two to three minutes. Flip the pancakes and cook for an additional one to two minutes, or until golden brown. Serve immediately with your favorite toppings.

While classic pancakes are delightful on their own, adding a twist can elevate them into something extraordinary. One popular variation is blueberry pancakes. Simply fold a cup of fresh or frozen blueberries into the batter before cooking. The blueberries burst with sweetness as they cook, creating pockets of juicy flavor throughout.

For a tropical touch, try banana pancakes. Thinly slice two ripe bananas and gently stir them into the batter. The bananas caramelize slightly during cooking, adding a natural sweetness that pairs beautifully with a drizzle of honey or a dollop of Greek yogurt.

Chocolate chip pancakes are a hit with kids and adults alike. Fold a half-cup of chocolate chips into the batter for a decadent treat. The chocolate melts into gooey pockets, making each bite a delightful indulgence. For an extra touch, sprinkle a few additional chocolate chips on top of the batter just before flipping the pancakes.

For those who enjoy a bit of spice, cinnamon pancakes are a wonderful option. Add one teaspoon of ground cinnamon to the dry ingredients before mixing the batter. The warm, aromatic spice adds depth and complexity to the pancakes, making them perfect for a cozy morning breakfast. Top with a sprinkle of powdered sugar and a dash of cinnamon for an extra special touch.

Savory variations of pancakes can also be a delightful surprise. Cheddar and chive pancakes, for example, are a delicious twist on the classic recipe. Add a cup of shredded sharp cheddar cheese and two tablespoons of finely chopped fresh chives to the batter. These pancakes pair wonderfully with sour cream and a side of crispy bacon.

For a heartier option, try incorporating whole grains into your pancakes. Substitute half of the all-purpose flour with whole wheat flour or oat flour. This not only adds a nutty flavor but also boosts the nutritional value of the pancakes. You can also add a handful of rolled oats or a tablespoon of flaxseeds for added texture and fiber.

Another way to vary your pancakes is by experimenting with different liquids in the batter. Substitute buttermilk for the regular milk to create buttermilk pancakes, which are known for their tangy flavor and tender crumb. If you're looking for a dairy-free option, almond milk or coconut milk can be used in place of cow's milk, each imparting its own unique flavor to the pancakes.

Playing with toppings is another way to bring variety to your pancake breakfasts. Fresh fruit like strawberries, raspberries, or sliced peaches add a burst of freshness and natural sweetness. For a decadent touch, try whipped cream and a drizzle of chocolate sauce. Nuts and seeds, such as chopped pecans, walnuts, or sunflower seeds, add a delightful crunch and a boost of protein.

Even the syrups and spreads you use can transform your pancakes. Traditional maple syrup is a classic choice, but honey, agave nectar, or fruit preserves offer delicious alternatives. Nut butters like peanut butter or almond butter spread over warm pancakes create a savory-sweet combination that is both satisfying and nutritious.

To ensure your pancakes are always a hit, consider a few additional tips and tricks. First, maintain a consistent cooking temperature. Too hot, and the pancakes will burn on the outside while remaining undercooked inside; too cool, and they will be pale and tough. Medium heat is generally ideal, but every stove varies, so adjust as needed.

Second, avoid overcrowding the skillet. Cooking too many pancakes at once can lower the temperature of the pan, resulting in uneven cooking. It's better to cook in smaller batches and keep the finished pancakes warm in a low oven until all are ready to serve.

Lastly, don't be afraid to experiment. Pancake batter is forgiving and versatile, providing a perfect canvas for culinary creativity. Whether you're adding fresh herbs, spices, or even savory ingredients like cooked bacon or sautéed vegetables, the possibilities are virtually endless.

Hearty Breakfast Casseroles

Hearty breakfast casseroles are the ultimate comfort food, perfect for feeding a crowd or ensuring you have a delicious meal ready to go on busy mornings.

These versatile dishes combine the best of breakfast into one convenient bake, often featuring eggs, cheese, meat, and vegetables all in one pan. The beauty of breakfast casseroles lies in their adaptability and ease of preparation, making them an ideal choice for both novice and experienced cooks.

A classic breakfast casserole starts with a base of eggs, which act as the binding agent for the other ingredients. To begin, preheat your oven to 350 degrees Fahrenheit and lightly grease a 9x13-inch baking dish. Crack a dozen large eggs into a large mixing bowl, then whisk them together until the yolks and whites are fully combined. Season the eggs with salt and pepper to taste. This basic egg mixture is the foundation upon which you can build a variety of casseroles.

One popular version is the sausage and cheese casserole. Start by browning a pound of breakfast sausage in a skillet over medium heat, breaking it up into small pieces as it cooks. Once the sausage is fully cooked, drain any excess fat and spread the sausage evenly in the prepared baking dish. Next, sprinkle two cups of shredded cheddar cheese over the sausage. Pour the egg mixture over the sausage and cheese, ensuring everything is evenly distributed. Bake the casserole in the preheated oven for 30 to 35 minutes, or until the eggs are set and the top is golden brown. Let it cool for a few minutes before slicing into squares and serving.

For a vegetarian option, consider a vegetable breakfast casserole. Begin by sautéing a medley of your favorite vegetables in a bit of olive oil until they are tender. Good choices include bell peppers, onions, mushrooms, spinach, and zucchini. Spread the cooked vegetables evenly in the greased baking dish. Instead of sausage, you can add a layer of cooked, diced potatoes or hash browns for a hearty texture. Sprinkle one and a half cups of shredded Swiss cheese over the vegetables and potatoes. Pour the egg mixture over the top and bake for the same amount of time as the sausage casserole. This version is not only flavorful but also packed with nutrients.

A breakfast casserole with a southwestern twist incorporates spicy chorizo, black beans, and salsa. Cook a pound of chorizo in a skillet until browned, then drain any excess grease. Spread the chorizo in the baking dish, followed by a can of drained and rinsed black beans. Add a cup of your favorite salsa and a cup of shredded Monterey Jack cheese. Pour the egg mixture over the layers and bake as directed. For an extra burst of flavor, top the casserole with chopped fresh cilantro and serve with a side of avocado slices or sour cream.

Another variation that is sure to please is the ham and cheese breakfast casserole. This version is particularly great for using up leftover holiday ham. Dice two cups of cooked ham and spread it in the baking dish. Add a layer of shredded sharp cheddar cheese and a handful of chopped green onions. Pour the egg mixture over the ham and cheese, then bake until set. This casserole is both savory and satisfying, making it a great option for brunch gatherings.

If you're looking to add a bit of sophistication to your breakfast casserole, consider a strata. A strata is essentially a savory bread pudding, made by layering bread cubes with other ingredients and soaking them in an egg mixture. To make a basic strata, cut a loaf of day-old bread into one-inch cubes and spread half of them in the greased baking dish. Add a layer of cooked bacon or sausage, sautéed vegetables, and shredded cheese. Top with the remaining bread cubes. Whisk together a dozen eggs, two cups of milk, and your preferred seasonings, then pour this mixture over the bread layers. Press down gently to ensure the bread absorbs the egg mixture. Cover the dish with plastic wrap and refrigerate for at least an hour, or overnight. Bake the strata at 350 degrees Fahrenheit for 45 to 50 minutes, or until the top is puffed and golden and the center is cooked through.

For those who enjoy a bit of sweetness in their breakfast, a French toast casserole is a delightful option. Start with a loaf of French bread or challah, cut into thick slices. Arrange the bread slices in the greased baking dish, overlapping slightly. In a mixing bowl, whisk together a dozen eggs, two cups of milk, half a cup of heavy cream, a teaspoon of vanilla extract, and a tablespoon of ground cinnamon. Pour this mixture over the bread, ensuring all the slices are well-coated. Cover and refrigerate for at least an hour, or overnight. Before baking, sprinkle the top with a mixture of brown sugar and cinnamon for a caramelized finish. Bake at 350 degrees Fahrenheit for 40 to 45 minutes, or until the top is golden and the custard is set. Serve with warm maple syrup and a dusting of powdered sugar for a truly decadent breakfast treat.

One practical advantage of breakfast casseroles is their make-ahead capability. Many casseroles can be assembled the night before and baked in the morning, making them perfect for busy weekdays or special occasions when you want to minimize morning prep work. Simply cover the assembled casserole with plastic wrap and refrigerate overnight. In the morning, remove the plastic wrap and bake as directed. This convenience allows you to enjoy a hearty, home-cooked breakfast with minimal effort.

Breakfast casseroles can also be customized to accommodate dietary preferences and restrictions. For a gluten-free version, use gluten-free bread or skip the bread altogether and add more vegetables or potatoes. Dairy-free casseroles can be made by using plant-based milk and cheese substitutes. For a lower-calorie option, use egg whites or egg substitutes and incorporate plenty of vegetables and lean proteins like turkey sausage or chicken.

Serving breakfast casseroles is a breeze, as they can be portioned into individual squares or slices, making them easy to serve and enjoy. Pair your casserole with a fresh fruit salad, yogurt, or a simple green salad for a well-rounded meal. Leftovers can be stored in the refrigerator for up to three days and reheated in the microwave or oven.

Warm and Wholesome Oatmeal

Oatmeal has long been a staple in many households, cherished for its versatility, nutritional benefits, and comforting warmth. When the mornings are chilly, or you simply need a nutritious start to your day, a bowl of warm and wholesome oatmeal can be just the ticket. This humble grain, often overlooked in favor of flashier breakfast options, offers a wealth of health benefits and can be prepared in countless ways to suit any palate.

To begin, let's talk about the different types of oats. The most common varieties you'll find in the grocery store are steel-cut oats, rolled oats, and instant oats. Steel-cut oats are the least processed, made by chopping whole oat groats into pieces. These have a chewy texture and a nutty flavor, requiring a longer cooking time, typically around 20-30 minutes. Rolled oats, also known as old-fashioned oats, are steamed and then rolled flat, making them quicker to cook than steel-cut oats, usually in about 5-10 minutes. Instant oats are pre-cooked and dried, making them the fastest option, often ready in just a minute or two after adding hot water or milk.

Choosing the right type of oat depends on your time constraints and texture preferences. For a hearty, chewy bowl of oatmeal, steel-cut oats are the way to go. If you prefer something quicker but still substantial, rolled oats are a great choice. Instant oats are perfect for those mornings when you're in a hurry but still want a nutritious meal.

Now, let's delve into the cooking process. A basic oatmeal recipe starts with a ratio of oats to liquid. For steel-cut oats, use one part oats to four parts water or milk. For rolled oats, the ratio is one part oats to two parts water or milk. Combine the oats and liquid in a saucepan, bring to a boil, then reduce the heat and simmer until the oats are tender and the mixture has thickened. Stir occasionally to prevent sticking and ensure even cooking.

The beauty of oatmeal lies in its customizability. Once you have your base, the possibilities for flavoring and topping your oatmeal are endless. A classic approach is to sweeten with a touch of brown sugar or maple syrup and top with fresh fruit. Sliced bananas, berries, or apples add natural sweetness and a burst of flavor. A sprinkle of nuts or seeds, such as almonds, walnuts, or chia seeds, provides a satisfying crunch and additional nutrients.

For those who enjoy a bit of spice, a dash of cinnamon, nutmeg, or even cardamom can elevate the flavor profile of your oatmeal. If you're feeling adventurous, try adding a spoonful of nut butter—peanut, almond, or cashew—for a rich, creamy texture and extra protein. A swirl of Greek yogurt can add tanginess and creaminess, making your oatmeal even more satisfying.

Savory oatmeal is an intriguing alternative to the traditional sweet preparation. Start with the same base of cooked oats, but instead of sweet toppings, think savory. Stir in a bit of grated cheese and top with a poached or fried egg for a breakfast that's reminiscent of risotto. Adding sautéed vegetables like spinach, mushrooms, or tomatoes can make your oatmeal a complete meal. A sprinkle of herbs such as chives, parsley, or basil can add freshness and a burst of flavor. For those who enjoy a bit of heat, a drizzle of hot sauce or a sprinkle of red pepper flakes can give your savory oatmeal a spicy kick.

Oatmeal isn't just for breakfast, either. It can be transformed into a delightful dessert. Consider making a warm oatmeal pudding by cooking oats with milk, a bit of sugar, and vanilla extract. Once thickened, top with a dollop of whipped cream and a sprinkle of cinnamon for a comforting dessert that's both wholesome and indulgent. Another option is baked oatmeal, which combines oats with eggs, milk, and your choice of sweeteners and mix-ins, then baked in the oven until set. This can be served warm, much like a bread pudding, and is perfect for a cozy evening treat or a make-ahead breakfast.

The nutritional benefits of oatmeal are impressive. Oats are a whole grain, meaning they retain all parts of the grain kernel, which makes them rich in fiber. This fiber, particularly beta-glucan, is known for its ability to lower cholesterol levels and promote heart health. Oats also have a low glycemic index, meaning they can help regulate blood sugar levels and provide sustained energy throughout the morning. Additionally, oats are a good source of essential vitamins and minerals, including manganese, phosphorus, magnesium, and iron.

For those with dietary restrictions, oatmeal is incredibly accommodating. It is naturally gluten-free, though it's important to purchase oats that are labeled as such to avoid cross-contamination. Oatmeal can easily be made vegan by using plant-based milk such as almond, soy, or oat milk. For those watching their sugar intake, oatmeal can be sweetened naturally with fruits or a small amount of honey or maple syrup.

Preparing oatmeal in advance is another fantastic way to enjoy this wholesome grain. Overnight oats have become a popular trend for good reason. Simply combine rolled oats with your choice of milk and any desired flavorings or mix-ins, then refrigerate overnight. The oats absorb the liquid and soften without the need for cooking. In the morning, you have a ready-to-eat, chilled oatmeal that can be enjoyed straight from the fridge or warmed up in the microwave. This method is perfect for busy mornings or for those who prefer a cold breakfast option.

Another make-ahead option is to batch-cook steel-cut oats. Cook a large pot of oats on the weekend, then portion them into individual servings and refrigerate or freeze. During the week, simply reheat a portion in the microwave, adding a bit of milk or water to reach the desired consistency. This ensures you have a quick and nutritious breakfast ready to go, even on the busiest of mornings.

Oatmeal's versatility extends beyond the bowl. Ground oats can be used as a flour substitute in baking, adding a nutty flavor and extra fiber to muffins, pancakes, and bread. Oat flour can often be used in place of all-purpose flour in many recipes, either partially or entirely, making it a great option for gluten-free baking. Additionally, oats can be used as a binder in meatballs or meatloaf, providing a healthier alternative to breadcrumbs.

Comforting Breakfast Bakes

When the morning light filters softly through kitchen windows, there's something inherently soothing about the aroma of a warm breakfast bake wafting through the house. Comforting breakfast bakes not only provide a delightful start to the day but also foster a sense of home and togetherness. Whether you're looking to feed a crowd or simply want to treat yourself to a cozy morning meal, breakfast bakes are an excellent choice due to their versatility, ease of preparation, and the ability to incorporate a variety of flavors and ingredients.

Breakfast bakes come in many forms, from sweet to savory, and can be easily adapted to suit individual preferences and dietary needs. A popular choice is the classic breakfast casserole, often brimming with eggs, cheese, and various fillings. To create a hearty egg-based bake, start with a dozen eggs whisked together with a splash of milk or cream. This forms the custard-like base that holds the casserole together. Season the eggs with salt, pepper, and perhaps a pinch of paprika or dried herbs for added depth.

Next, consider the fillings. Breakfast casseroles are wonderfully flexible, accommodating whatever you have on hand. Sautéed vegetables such as bell peppers, onions, spinach, and mushrooms add color, texture, and nutrition. For protein, cooked bacon, sausage, or ham are traditional favorites, though vegetarian options like black beans or tofu can be equally delicious. Grated cheese, whether sharp cheddar, Swiss, or feta, melts into the casserole, creating pockets of gooey goodness.

To assemble, layer the fillings in a greased baking dish, pour the egg mixture over the top, and sprinkle with more cheese if desired. Bake in a preheated oven at 350°F (175°C) for about 30-40 minutes, or until the eggs are set and the top is golden brown.

Allow the casserole to cool slightly before slicing into generous portions. This dish can be prepared the night before and baked in the morning, making it perfect for busy weekdays or leisurely weekends.

For those with a sweet tooth, baked oatmeal is a comforting alternative that combines the heartiness of oats with the warmth of a freshly baked treat. Start with rolled oats as the base, mixing them with milk, eggs, and a touch of sweetener such as brown sugar or maple syrup. Add-ins can range from fresh or dried fruit—think berries, apples, or raisins—to nuts and seeds for added texture and flavor. Spices like cinnamon, nutmeg, and vanilla extract enhance the sweetness and aroma.

Combine the wet and dry ingredients, pour into a greased baking dish, and bake at 350°F (175°C) for 30-40 minutes, or until the top is set and the edges are slightly crisp. Baked oatmeal can be made in large batches, stored in the refrigerator, and reheated as needed, providing a quick and nutritious breakfast throughout the week. Serve it warm, with a splash of milk or a dollop of yogurt, and perhaps a drizzle of honey or a spoonful of fruit preserves.

Another delightful option is a breakfast strata, which layers bread, eggs, cheese, and other ingredients similarly to a savory bread pudding. Day-old bread works best, as it absorbs the egg mixture without becoming too soggy. Cut the bread into cubes and layer in a greased baking dish with sautéed vegetables, cooked meats, and cheese. Whisk together eggs and milk, season with salt and pepper, and pour over the layered ingredients. Press down gently to ensure the bread absorbs the liquid.

Cover the dish with foil and refrigerate for at least an hour, or overnight, allowing the flavors to meld. When ready to bake, preheat the oven to 350°F (175°C), bake covered for 30 minutes, then uncover and bake for an additional 15-20 minutes, or until the top is golden and the custard is set. A strata can be customized with different flavor profiles, such as Mediterranean with spinach, feta, and sun-dried tomatoes, or Southwestern with chorizo, black beans, and cheddar.

For a more indulgent treat, consider a French toast bake. This dish transforms the classic breakfast favorite into a crowd-pleasing casserole. Use thick slices of bread, such as brioche or challah, which hold up well to soaking. Arrange the bread in a greased baking dish, overlapping slightly. In a separate bowl, whisk together eggs, milk, cream, sugar, and vanilla extract. Pour the mixture over the bread, ensuring it is evenly soaked. For added flair, sprinkle with cinnamon, nutmeg, and perhaps a handful of fresh berries or chopped nuts.

Cover and refrigerate the dish overnight, allowing the bread to absorb the custard. In the morning, preheat the oven to 350°F (175°C) and bake for 45-50 minutes, or until the top is puffed and golden. Serve the French toast bake warm, with a dusting of powdered sugar, a drizzle of maple syrup, or a spoonful of fruit compote.

Breakfast bakes offer a wonderful opportunity to experiment with flavors and ingredients, making them suitable for any occasion. They are particularly well-suited for gatherings, as they can be prepared in advance and baked just before serving, allowing you to enjoy the company of your guests without being tied to the kitchen. Additionally, these dishes are often hearty enough to keep you satisfied until lunchtime, making them a practical choice for busy mornings.

For those who enjoy meal prepping, breakfast bakes are a game-changer. They can be portioned into individual servings, making it easy to grab a nutritious breakfast on the go. Whether you prefer the savory richness of an egg casserole, the comforting sweetness of baked oatmeal, the layered goodness of a strata, or the indulgence of a French toast bake, there's a breakfast bake to suit every taste and occasion.

Savory Morning Muffins

Savory morning muffins offer a delightful departure from their sweeter counterparts, providing a hearty and flavorful start to your day. These muffins combine the convenience of a portable breakfast with the satisfying elements of a full meal, featuring ingredients like cheese, vegetables, and proteins. They are perfect for busy mornings, leisurely brunches, or even as a quick snack throughout the day. The versatility of savory muffins allows for endless combinations, making them a staple recipe that can be tailored to individual tastes and dietary preferences.

The foundation of any good muffin is its base batter. For savory muffins, this typically includes flour, baking powder, eggs, milk, and oil or melted butter. The choice of flour can vary depending on dietary needs—while all-purpose flour is standard, whole wheat or gluten-free alternatives like almond or oat flour can also be used. Baking powder acts as the leavening agent, giving the muffins their rise and fluffy texture. Eggs provide structure and moisture, while milk and oil add richness and tenderness to the crumb.

Begin by preheating your oven to 375°F (190°C) and lining a muffin tin with paper liners or greasing it well. In a large bowl, whisk together the dry ingredients: 2 cups of flour, 1 tablespoon of baking powder, and a pinch of salt. In a separate bowl, combine the wet ingredients: 2 large eggs, 1 cup of milk, and 1/4 cup of oil or melted butter. Mix the wet ingredients into the dry ingredients just until combined—overmixing can lead to dense muffins.

The beauty of savory muffins lies in the variety of mix-ins you can incorporate. Cheese is a popular addition, offering a burst of flavor and a gooey texture when melted. Cheddar, feta, Parmesan, and goat cheese are all excellent choices. Grate or crumble about 1 to 1 1/2 cups of cheese and fold it into the batter. For a balanced flavor profile, consider adding sautéed vegetables like bell peppers, onions, spinach, or zucchini. These not only contribute flavor but also add moisture and nutrients. Sauté the vegetables in a bit of oil until tender, then let them cool slightly before mixing them into the batter.

Proteins such as cooked bacon, sausage, or ham can also be delicious additions. Chop these into small pieces and fold them in, ensuring they are evenly distributed throughout the batter. For a vegetarian option, consider adding beans, tofu, or tempeh. Fresh or dried herbs like chives, parsley, dill, or thyme can enhance the flavor even further. A teaspoon or two of your favorite herbs can make a significant difference in the taste profile of your muffins.

Spoon the batter into the prepared muffin tin, filling each cup about three-quarters full. This allows room for the muffins to rise without overflowing. If desired, sprinkle a bit of extra cheese or herbs on top of each muffin for added visual appeal and flavor. Bake in the preheated oven for 20-25 minutes, or until a toothpick inserted into the center of a muffin comes out clean. Let the muffins cool in the tin for a few minutes before transferring them to a wire rack to cool completely.

Savory muffins are incredibly versatile and can be customized to suit various dietary needs. For a gluten-free version, substitute the all-purpose flour with a gluten-free blend or almond flour. If you're looking to reduce the fat content, use Greek yogurt or applesauce in place of oil or butter. To make the muffins dairy-free, opt for plant-based milk and cheese alternatives. The options are endless, allowing you to create a muffin that meets your specific dietary requirements without sacrificing flavor.

These muffins can be enjoyed warm or at room temperature, making them an excellent option for meal prep. Store them in an airtight container at room temperature for up to two days, or in the refrigerator for up to a week. For longer storage, individually wrap the muffins and freeze them for up to three months. Simply reheat in the microwave or oven before serving.

One of the most enjoyable aspects of making savory muffins is experimenting with different flavor combinations. Here are a few ideas to get you started:

1. **Cheddar and Chive**: Combine sharp cheddar cheese with fresh chives for a classic and flavorful muffin.

2. **Spinach and Feta**: Mix sautéed spinach and crumbled feta cheese for a Mediterranean-inspired treat.

3. **Bacon and Cheddar**: Add crispy bacon bits and cheddar cheese for a hearty, protein-packed muffin.

4. **Sun-Dried Tomato and Basil**: Incorporate chopped sun-dried tomatoes and fresh basil for a burst of Italian flavor.

5. **Zucchini and Parmesan**: Grate zucchini and mix with Parmesan cheese for a moist, savory muffin.

Savory muffins are not only delicious but also a great way to use up leftover ingredients. Have some extra roasted vegetables or cooked meat from dinner? Toss them into the muffin batter for a new and exciting breakfast option. The adaptability of these muffins makes them perfect for minimizing food waste while creating a variety of tasty meals.

Moreover, savory muffins can be a fun and engaging cooking project with children. Kids can help with mixing the batter, choosing their favorite ingredients, and filling the muffin tins. This hands-on activity can foster a love for cooking and encourage healthier eating habits by involving them in the kitchen.

For those who enjoy hosting brunches or breakfast gatherings, savory muffins are a fantastic addition to the menu. They can be made ahead of time, freeing you up to focus on other dishes or simply enjoy the company of your guests. Pair them with fresh fruit, yogurt, and a hot beverage for a well-rounded and satisfying meal.

Chapter 3

Soul-Soothing Soups

Chicken Noodle Soup

Chicken noodle soup is a beloved classic that transcends generations and cultures. Its warm, comforting nature makes it a go-to remedy for chilly days and sniffly noses, and its simplicity ensures it can be made by cooks of all skill levels. The beauty of chicken noodle soup lies in its flexibility; it can be as straightforward or as complex as you desire, with endless variations to suit every palate. This chapter delves into the essential components of a great chicken noodle soup, tips for perfecting your technique, and creative ways to customize the recipe.

The foundation of any good chicken noodle soup is its broth. A rich, flavorful broth serves as the base of the soup, infusing every spoonful with depth and warmth. While store-bought broth can be convenient, making your own from scratch elevates the soup to new heights. Start with a whole chicken or a combination of bone-in chicken pieces, such as thighs and drumsticks, which offer a balance of meat and bone for a robust flavor.

Place the chicken in a large stockpot and cover with cold water, ensuring the water level is about two inches above the chicken. Add aromatics like a halved onion, a couple of carrots, celery stalks, garlic cloves, and a bouquet garni (a bundle of fresh herbs such as thyme, parsley, and bay leaves tied together with kitchen twine). Bring the pot to a gentle simmer over medium heat, skimming off any foam that rises to the surface. Reduce the heat to low and let it simmer for about 1.5 to 2 hours, or until the chicken is tender and the broth is rich and fragrant.

Once the broth is ready, carefully remove the chicken and set it aside to cool slightly. Strain the broth through a fine-mesh sieve into another large pot, discarding the solids. If time allows, refrigerate the broth to let the fat rise to the top, making it easier to skim off for a clearer soup. Alternatively, use a fat separator to achieve the same result.

While the broth is cooling, prepare the vegetables for the soup. Classic choices include diced carrots, celery, and onions, creating a mirepoix that forms the flavor base. Sauté the vegetables in a bit of olive oil or butter in a large pot over medium heat until they begin to soften, about 5-7 minutes. This step enhances their natural sweetness and adds complexity to the soup.

Shred the cooled chicken, discarding the skin and bones, and add the meat to the pot with the sautéed vegetables. Pour the strained broth over the chicken and vegetables, bringing the mixture to a gentle simmer. Season with salt and pepper to taste, and let the soup simmer for about 20 minutes, allowing the flavors to meld.

Noodles are a crucial component of chicken noodle soup, providing heartiness and texture. Egg noodles are traditional, but any pasta shape can work. Cook the noodles separately according to the package instructions, then add them to the soup just before serving. This prevents the noodles from becoming overly soft and absorbing too much broth.

For a touch of brightness, finish the soup with a squeeze of fresh lemon juice and a sprinkle of chopped fresh herbs like parsley or dill. These additions lift the flavors and add a fresh, vibrant note to the comforting dish.

Chicken noodle soup is highly customizable, with numerous variations to suit different tastes and dietary preferences. For a gluten-free option, use rice noodles or gluten-free pasta. To make the soup heartier, consider adding other vegetables like peas, corn, or spinach. For an Asian-inspired twist, incorporate ingredients like ginger, soy sauce, and bok choy, and swap the egg noodles for udon or soba noodles.

In addition to its flavor and versatility, chicken noodle soup is cherished for its potential health benefits. It's often turned to as a remedy for colds and flu, thanks to its hydrating broth, nutritious ingredients, and the soothing warmth it provides. The steam from the hot soup can help clear nasal congestion, while the chicken offers protein and the vegetables supply essential vitamins and minerals.

For those who enjoy meal prepping, chicken noodle soup is a perfect candidate. It can be made in large batches and stored in the refrigerator for up to five days or frozen for up to three months. When reheating, it's best to warm the soup gently on the stovetop to maintain the integrity of the ingredients.

Beyond its practical benefits, chicken noodle soup carries a sense of nostalgia and comfort. Many people have fond memories of enjoying a bowl of this soup made by a loved one, often when they were feeling under the weather. The act of making chicken noodle soup can be a nurturing experience, whether you're preparing it for yourself, your family, or friends.

For those new to cooking, chicken noodle soup is an excellent recipe to start with. It teaches fundamental skills like making broth, sautéing vegetables, and balancing flavors. As you become more comfortable with the basic recipe, you can experiment with different ingredients and techniques, building your confidence in the kitchen.

One of the most rewarding aspects of making chicken noodle soup is sharing it with others. Whether you're bringing a pot to a sick friend, serving it at a family gathering, or simply enjoying it at home, this soup has a way of bringing people together. Its comforting nature and delicious taste make it a universally loved dish that transcends cultural boundaries.

Creamy Tomato Basil Soup

Tomato soup is a timeless classic, but when you add a creamy texture and the aromatic essence of basil, it transforms into a comforting, luxurious dish that feels both familiar and sophisticated. Creamy tomato basil soup is perfect for any season, offering a warm, rich bowl in the winter and a vibrant, fresh taste in the summer. This chapter will guide you through creating a perfect creamy tomato basil soup from scratch, highlighting important techniques, tips for customization, and ways to elevate the flavor to suit any occasion.

The heart of this soup lies in the quality of the tomatoes. While canned tomatoes are convenient and can produce excellent results, using fresh, ripe tomatoes when they are in season can elevate your soup to a whole new level. Roma tomatoes are often preferred for their robust flavor and lower water content, but any ripe, juicy variety will work.

To start, prepare the tomatoes. If using fresh tomatoes, you will need to peel and seed them. Begin by scoring a small "X" on the bottom of each tomato with a sharp knife and then blanch them in boiling water for about 30 seconds. Transfer the tomatoes to an ice bath to cool, then peel away the skins, which should slip off easily. Cut the tomatoes in half, scoop out the seeds, and roughly chop the flesh.

In a large pot, heat a couple of tablespoons of olive oil or butter over medium heat. Add a diced onion and cook until it becomes translucent, about 5-7 minutes. The onion provides a sweet, savory base that complements the acidity of the tomatoes. Add minced garlic and cook for another minute until fragrant. Be careful not to burn the garlic, as it can become bitter.

Next, add the prepared tomatoes (or two large cans of whole tomatoes if using canned) to the pot, along with their juices. For an extra depth of flavor, consider adding a tablespoon of tomato paste, which will enhance the tomato essence and add a slight sweetness. Stir in a pinch of sugar to balance the acidity, especially if the tomatoes are very tart, and season with salt and freshly ground black pepper to taste.

To build more complexity, you can add a splash of vegetable or chicken broth. This not only thins out the soup slightly but also infuses it with additional layers of flavor. For a heartier, more rustic soup, you can leave the mixture chunky, or you can opt for a smoother texture by blending it. If blending, allow the soup to cool slightly before transferring it to a blender or using an immersion blender directly in the pot. Blend until smooth, taking care to avoid splashes of hot liquid.

Return the blended soup to the pot and bring it to a gentle simmer. At this stage, add the key ingredient that transforms this from a simple tomato soup to a creamy delight: heavy cream. Slowly stir in about a cup of heavy cream, adjusting the amount to achieve your desired level of creaminess. For a lighter option, you can use half-and-half or even coconut milk, which adds a subtle, exotic flavor twist.

Now, it's time for the basil. Fresh basil leaves are essential for this soup, providing a fragrant, slightly peppery note that pairs beautifully with the sweetness of the tomatoes and the richness of the cream. Chiffonade a generous handful of basil leaves by stacking them, rolling them into a tight cylinder, and slicing thinly. Stir the basil into the soup just before serving to retain its vibrant color and flavor.

To enhance the presentation and add a touch of elegance, drizzle a bit of extra virgin olive oil over each bowl of soup and garnish with a few whole basil leaves or a dollop of crème fraîche. A sprinkle of freshly grated Parmesan cheese can also add a savory, umami kick.

Creamy tomato basil soup is incredibly versatile and can be customized in numerous ways to suit your taste or dietary preferences. For a vegan version, substitute the heavy cream with a plant-based milk such as almond or oat milk, and ensure the broth is vegetable-based. You can also add other vegetables, such as roasted red peppers, for a smoky depth, or carrots and celery for additional sweetness and texture.

Serving this soup with a side of crusty bread or a classic grilled cheese sandwich makes for a comforting and satisfying meal. The contrast of the creamy, tangy soup with the crispy, buttery bread creates a delightful combination that is hard to resist.

For those who enjoy a bit of spice, consider adding a pinch of red pepper flakes or a dash of hot sauce to the soup. This can provide a pleasant heat that complements the rich, creamy base. Similarly, a splash of balsamic vinegar or a squeeze of lemon juice can brighten the flavors and add a touch of acidity to balance the creaminess.

Storing creamy tomato basil soup is simple, making it a great option for meal prep. It can be refrigerated in an airtight container for up to five days. When reheating, do so gently over low heat to maintain the smooth texture and prevent the cream from curdling. This soup also freezes well; portion it into individual containers for easy, ready-to-heat meals. Just remember to leave out the basil until just before serving to keep its fresh flavor intact.

Creating a creamy tomato basil soup from scratch is a rewarding experience that showcases the beauty of simple, fresh ingredients. It's a dish that invites you to slow down and savor the process, from peeling the tomatoes to stirring in the fragrant basil. Whether you're making it for a family dinner, a cozy lunch, or a special occasion, this soup brings warmth and comfort to the table.

Hearty Beef Stew

Beef stew is a timeless dish that embodies the essence of comfort food. Its rich, savory aroma fills the kitchen, creating a sense of warmth and coziness. Perfect for chilly days, hearty beef stew is a meal that nourishes the body and soul, bringing together simple ingredients to create a complex, deeply satisfying flavor. This chapter will guide you through the steps of making a classic hearty beef stew from scratch, offering tips for perfecting the technique and suggestions for variations to suit different tastes.

The cornerstone of an excellent beef stew is, naturally, the beef. Choose a cut that benefits from slow cooking, such as chuck roast or brisket. These cuts are marbled with fat and connective tissue that break down during cooking, resulting in tender, flavorful meat. Begin by cutting the beef into 1-2 inch cubes, ensuring uniformity for even cooking.

Season the beef cubes generously with salt and pepper. This initial seasoning layer is crucial for developing depth of flavor. In a large, heavy-bottomed pot or Dutch oven, heat a few tablespoons of oil over medium-high heat. When the oil is shimmering, add the beef in batches, taking care not to overcrowd the pot. Browning the meat is a vital step; it caramelizes the surface and locks in juices, adding a rich, savory foundation to your stew.

Once all the beef is browned, transfer it to a plate and set aside.

In the same pot, add a bit more oil if necessary and sauté a mirepoix of diced onions, carrots, and celery. These vegetables form the aromatic base of the stew, contributing sweetness and complexity. Cook the mirepoix over medium heat until the onions are translucent and the vegetables are beginning to soften, about 5-7 minutes. Incorporate minced garlic and cook for an additional minute, until fragrant.

To deepen the flavor, deglaze the pot with a splash of red wine or beef broth, scraping up the browned bits from the bottom of the pot. This step is essential for incorporating all the flavorful residues left by the beef. Return the browned beef to the pot, along with any accumulated juices.

Next, add the main liquid component. A combination of beef broth and red wine works wonderfully, with the wine adding a rich, robust flavor. For a more traditional approach, simply use beef broth. You'll need enough liquid to cover the beef and vegetables, typically about 4 cups of broth and 1 cup of wine. Add a couple of bay leaves, a few sprigs of fresh thyme, and a tablespoon of tomato paste for added depth. The tomato paste not only enriches the stew but also helps thicken the sauce as it simmers.

Bring the stew to a boil, then reduce the heat to low, cover, and let it simmer gently. The key to a perfect beef stew is patience; allowing it to cook slowly ensures the meat becomes tender and the flavors meld beautifully. Plan for at least two hours of simmering, checking occasionally and stirring to prevent sticking.

About halfway through the cooking time, add chunks of potatoes and additional carrots. These vegetables absorb the flavors of the stew and provide a hearty, comforting texture. If you prefer other root vegetables like parsnips or turnips, feel free to include them as well. Maintain a slow simmer, ensuring the vegetables cook through without becoming mushy.

Towards the end of the cooking process, taste the stew and adjust the seasoning with salt and pepper as needed. For a thicker consistency, you can create a slurry by mixing a tablespoon of flour or cornstarch with a bit of cold water and stirring it into the stew. Allow it to cook for a few more minutes until the stew has thickened to your liking.

For a final touch, consider adding a handful of frozen peas or chopped parsley just before serving. The peas add a pop of color and sweetness, while parsley contributes a fresh, herbal note that brightens the dish.

Hearty beef stew is incredibly versatile and can be customized to your preference. For a bit of heat, add a pinch of red pepper flakes or a dash of hot sauce. To enhance the umami flavor, a splash of Worcestershire sauce or soy sauce can be incorporated. For a more Mediterranean twist, include olives and a sprinkle of rosemary.

Serving beef stew is as enjoyable as making it. Ladle the stew into bowls and enjoy it with crusty bread or over a bed of creamy mashed potatoes. The bread is perfect for soaking up the rich, flavorful broth, while the mashed potatoes add an extra layer of comfort.

Storing leftover stew is simple and convenient. It can be refrigerated for up to four days or frozen for up to three months. When reheating, do so gently over low heat to maintain the texture of the meat and vegetables.

Beyond its deliciousness, beef stew carries a sense of tradition and nostalgia. It's a dish that has been passed down through generations, each cook adding their unique touch. Making beef stew from scratch allows you to connect with this culinary heritage, creating new memories and traditions in the process.

For beginners, beef stew is a fantastic recipe to master. It teaches essential cooking techniques like browning meat, deglazing, and simmering, which are foundational skills in the kitchen. The process of making stew is also forgiving, allowing you to experiment with different flavors and ingredients without fear of failure.

Classic French Onion Soup

French onion soup is a dish that captures the essence of French culinary tradition, combining simplicity with deep, sophisticated flavors. Its origins are humble, rooted in the kitchens of 18th-century France, where it was considered a meal for the poor due to the availability and affordability of its main ingredients: onions and broth. Today, however, it is celebrated worldwide, often appearing on the menus of fine dining establishments. This chapter delves into creating a classic French onion soup, guiding you through each step with practical advice to ensure your soup is rich, comforting, and unforgettable.

The soul of French onion soup lies in its caramelized onions. The slow, careful caramelization process transforms the onions from sharp and pungent to sweet and deeply flavorful, creating the backbone of the soup. Begin by selecting the right onions; yellow onions are traditionally used for their balanced sweetness and robustness, but a mix of yellow and sweet Vidalia onions can add complexity.

Start by slicing the onions thinly. You will need about six large onions to make a substantial pot of soup. Heat a generous amount of butter in a large, heavy-bottomed pot over medium heat. Once the butter has melted and is beginning to foam, add the onions. Stir to coat them evenly in the butter, then reduce the heat to low. The key to caramelizing onions is patience—this process can take upwards of 45 minutes to an hour. Stir the onions occasionally, allowing them to develop a deep golden brown color gradually. Be careful not to rush this step, as properly caramelized onions are crucial for the soup's depth of flavor.

As the onions cook, their natural sugars break down and caramelize, creating a rich, sweet base. If the onions begin to stick to the pot or cook too quickly, add a splash of water or a bit more butter to prevent burning. Season the onions with a pinch of salt to help draw out their moisture and enhance their sweetness.

Once the onions have reached a deep, golden brown color and have a jam-like consistency, it's time to deglaze the pot. This step involves adding liquid to lift the flavorful browned bits stuck to the bottom of the pot, known as the fond. Traditionally, a dry white wine is used for deglazing, adding a subtle acidity that balances the sweetness of the onions. Pour in about half a cup of wine and stir, scraping up any stuck-on bits. Allow the wine to simmer until it has mostly evaporated, intensifying the flavors.

Next, add beef broth to the pot. High-quality broth is essential; it provides the soup with body and richness. You will need about six to eight cups of broth, enough to fully cover the onions and create a hearty soup. For an extra layer of flavor, you can add a splash of brandy or cognac along with the broth. Bring the mixture to a boil, then reduce the heat and let it simmer gently for about 30 minutes. This allows the flavors to meld and the soup to develop its characteristic richness.

To season the soup, add a bouquet garni—a bundle of fresh herbs such as thyme, parsley, and a bay leaf—tied together with kitchen twine. This imparts a subtle herbal note without overpowering the soup. Season with salt and freshly ground black pepper to taste. As the soup simmers, taste and adjust the seasoning, ensuring a balanced flavor profile.

While the soup simmers, prepare the iconic topping: slices of toasted baguette and melted cheese. Slice a baguette into rounds and toast them until golden and crisp. Traditional French onion soup uses Gruyère cheese for its nutty, slightly sweet flavor and excellent melting properties. You can also use a combination of Gruyère and Swiss cheese or even add a bit of Parmesan for extra depth.

When the soup is ready, preheat your oven's broiler. Ladle the soup into oven-safe bowls, leaving some room at the top for the bread and cheese. Place a slice or two of the toasted baguette on top of each bowl of soup, then generously sprinkle with grated cheese. Arrange the bowls on a baking sheet for easier handling and broil until the cheese is melted, bubbly, and golden brown. This final step creates a deliciously gooey, crisp topping that contrasts beautifully with the rich, savory soup beneath.

Serve the French onion soup immediately, ensuring each bowl has a perfect balance of broth, caramelized onions, toasted bread, and melted cheese. The first spoonful should offer a symphony of flavors and textures: the sweet, tender onions, the robust broth, the crunchy bread, and the creamy, melted cheese.

French onion soup is not only a treat for the taste buds but also a visually appealing dish. The golden, bubbling cheese and the deep, inviting color of the broth make for a stunning presentation. It's a perfect dish for a cozy dinner on a cold evening, offering warmth and comfort in every bite.

While the classic recipe is a masterpiece in its own right, there are ways to personalize and enhance your

French onion soup. For a richer, more decadent version, you can add a splash of heavy cream or a dollop of crème fraîche just before serving. If you prefer a vegetarian option, use vegetable broth instead of beef broth and incorporate a bit of soy sauce or miso paste to add umami depth.

Storing French onion soup is straightforward, making it an excellent option for meal prep. The soup itself can be made ahead of time and stored in the refrigerator for up to four days. When ready to serve, reheat the soup on the stovetop and prepare the bread and cheese topping fresh. The soup also freezes well; portion it into individual containers without the bread and cheese for easy, reheatable meals.

For those looking to elevate their French onion soup further, consider experimenting with different types of onions or adding other ingredients like roasted garlic or a splash of balsamic vinegar. These additions can introduce new flavors while maintaining the soup's traditional essence.

Seasonal Vegetable Soups

Seasonal vegetable soups celebrate the bounty of each season, turning fresh, local produce into vibrant, nourishing meals. These soups are not only delicious but also highlight the importance of eating seasonally, which ensures that ingredients are at their peak flavor and nutritional value. Crafting a seasonal vegetable soup involves understanding the unique characteristics of each season's produce and how to best bring out their flavors in a comforting bowl of soup.

Spring, with its promise of renewal, brings a variety of fresh, tender vegetables that are perfect for light, refreshing soups. As the earth awakens, delicate greens, peas, asparagus, and young carrots make their debut. A classic spring vegetable soup might start with a fragrant base of leeks and garlic, sautéed in a bit of olive oil until soft. To this, add sliced asparagus, peas, and baby carrots, allowing them to sauté briefly before covering with a light vegetable broth. A touch of lemon zest and juice brightens the flavors, while a handful of fresh herbs like dill, parsley, or mint adds a burst of freshness. Simmer until the vegetables are tender but still vibrant, and finish with a swirl of crème fraîche or a dollop of Greek yogurt for a creamy contrast.

Summer soups take advantage of the abundant, sun-ripened produce that bursts forth in warm weather. Think tomatoes, bell peppers, zucchini, and corn. A chilled gazpacho is a quintessential summer soup, requiring no cooking and capturing the essence of garden-fresh tomatoes. Start by blending ripe tomatoes with cucumbers, red bell peppers, red onions, garlic, and a splash of red wine vinegar. Olive oil is drizzled in to emulsify the mixture, giving it a silky texture. Season with salt, pepper, and a hint of cayenne for a mild kick. Serve this vibrant soup chilled, garnished with diced vegetables, croutons, and a drizzle of olive oil. Alternatively, a corn chowder made with sweet summer corn, potatoes, and a touch of cream can be a comforting yet light dish for cooler summer evenings.

As the air turns crisp and leaves begin to fall, autumn brings a harvest of robust, earthy vegetables perfect for heartier soups. Squash, pumpkins, sweet potatoes, and root vegetables like parsnips and turnips come into their own. A roasted butternut squash soup captures the essence of fall with its rich, sweet flavor. Begin by roasting cubed squash with a drizzle of olive oil, salt, and pepper until caramelized and tender. In a large pot, sauté onions, garlic, and a pinch of nutmeg until fragrant. Add the roasted squash and cover with vegetable broth. Simmer for 20 minutes, then puree until smooth. Stir in a splash of apple cider or a touch of cream to enhance the sweetness and provide a silky finish. Garnish with toasted pumpkin seeds for a crunchy contrast.

Winter's chill calls for soups that are deeply warming and nourishing, utilizing the hearty greens and root vegetables that thrive in colder months. Cabbage, kale, potatoes, and carrots become the stars of hearty, sustaining soups. A classic minestrone, packed with winter vegetables and beans, is a perfect example. Start by sautéing onions, garlic, and celery in olive oil until soft. Add diced carrots, potatoes, and a can of diced tomatoes, followed by vegetable broth. Include a handful of dark leafy greens like kale or Swiss chard, and a can of cannellini beans for added protein and texture. Season with bay leaves, thyme, and rosemary, and let the soup simmer until all the vegetables are tender. Finish with a handful of pasta or rice and cook until al dente. Serve with a generous grating of Parmesan cheese and a drizzle of good olive oil.

Crafting seasonal vegetable soups not only highlights the best of what each season has to offer but also supports local agriculture and sustainable eating practices. By focusing on what's available locally, you reduce the carbon footprint associated with transporting out-of-season produce and enjoy ingredients at their freshest and most flavorful.

To make the most of your vegetable soups, consider these preparation tips. First, always start with the freshest ingredients you can find. Visit local farmers' markets or join a CSA (Community Supported Agriculture) to get the best seasonal produce. Second, don't be afraid to experiment with different herbs and spices. Fresh herbs like basil, cilantro, and mint can add a fresh, vibrant note, while spices like cumin, coriander, and cinnamon can add warmth and complexity. Third, consider the texture of your soup. Pureeing part or all of the soup can create a creamy, luxurious texture without the need for cream, making it lighter and healthier.

Another key element is the broth. While store-bought broth is convenient, making your own vegetable broth can significantly enhance the flavor of your soups. Save vegetable scraps like onion skins, carrot tops, and celery leaves, and simmer them with water, bay leaves, and peppercorns for a rich, homemade broth. This not only reduces waste but also ensures that your broth is free from preservatives and excess sodium.

For added depth of flavor, consider roasting your vegetables before adding them to the soup. Roasting concentrates their natural sugars and adds a layer of caramelized complexity. This technique works particularly well with root vegetables and squash.

In addition to seasonal vegetables, don't overlook the potential of adding grains and legumes to your soups. Barley, farro, lentils, and beans can turn a simple vegetable soup into a complete, hearty meal. They add texture, protein, and fiber, making your soups more satisfying and nutritious.

Seasonal vegetable soups can also be a great way to incorporate more plant-based meals into your diet.

They are naturally vegetarian or vegan, and by focusing on the quality and variety of vegetables, you can create dishes that are both flavorful and fulfilling.

Moreover, these soups are excellent for meal prep. Most vegetable soups store well in the refrigerator for several days and can also be frozen for longer storage. Batch cooking a large pot of soup can provide you with ready-made meals that are easy to reheat, saving time on busy days. When reheating, add a splash of broth or water to restore the soup's consistency, as it may thicken as it cools.

Chapter 4

Homestyle Main Dishes

Classic Meatloaf with a Twist

Meatloaf has been a staple in American kitchens for generations, a comforting dish that conjures images of family dinners and home-cooked warmth. However, the beauty of meatloaf lies not just in its familiarity but in its versatility. With a few creative adjustments, this classic can be elevated to new culinary heights, offering a fresh take while retaining its beloved core. Here, we'll explore a unique version of classic meatloaf that incorporates unexpected ingredients to add depth and complexity, making it an unforgettable centerpiece for any meal.

Start by selecting the right blend of meats. Traditional meatloaf often uses a combination of ground beef, pork, and veal. This trio creates a balanced flavor profile and ensures a juicy texture. For our twist, consider incorporating ground turkey or lamb for a different taste experience. Ground turkey, with its leaner profile, lends a lighter texture, while lamb introduces a rich, slightly gamey flavor that pairs beautifully with robust seasonings.

The foundation of any great meatloaf is the seasoning. Classic recipes rely on staples like onions, garlic, and Worcestershire sauce. To infuse new life into the dish, we'll add finely chopped sun-dried tomatoes and a handful of crumbled feta cheese. The sun-dried tomatoes provide a concentrated burst of umami and sweetness, while the feta adds a tangy, creamy note that melts into the meat, enhancing its richness.

Binding the meatloaf is crucial for achieving the right texture. Traditional recipes often use breadcrumbs soaked in milk or eggs. For a healthier and gluten-free option, try using cooked quinoa or oats instead. Quinoa not only binds the meat but also adds a subtle nuttiness and a boost of protein. Meanwhile, oats provide a similar binding effect with a slightly heartier texture. Both alternatives contribute to a moist, cohesive loaf without the heaviness of breadcrumbs.

Herbs and spices are where you can truly personalize your meatloaf. While parsley and thyme are classic choices, incorporating fresh basil and oregano can impart a Mediterranean flair. For a more exotic variation, consider adding ground cumin and coriander, which bring a warm, earthy complexity. A touch of smoked paprika can also add a hint of smokiness that complements the meat beautifully.

The glaze is another opportunity to innovate. Instead of the standard ketchup or tomato-based glaze, experiment with a balsamic reduction or a mixture of hoisin sauce and sriracha for a sweet and spicy kick. A balsamic reduction, with its syrupy consistency and deep, tangy flavor, can be brushed over the meatloaf before baking, creating a caramelized crust that contrasts the savory interior. Alternatively, the hoisin-sriracha mixture adds an Asian-inspired twist, balancing sweetness with heat and giving the meatloaf a glossy, appetizing finish.

To assemble the meatloaf, gently mix your chosen meats with the sun-dried tomatoes, feta, quinoa or oats, herbs, and spices. Be careful not to overwork the mixture, as this can result in a dense, tough loaf. Shape the mixture into a loaf on a lined baking sheet or press it into a loaf pan for a more uniform shape. Brush the top with your selected glaze and bake at

350°F (175°C) until the internal temperature reaches 160°F (71°C), typically around an hour.

While the meatloaf bakes, consider preparing complementary side dishes that echo its flavors. Roasted vegetables, such as carrots, parsnips, and Brussels sprouts, can be tossed with olive oil and the same herbs used in the meatloaf, then roasted until caramelized and tender. A simple side salad with mixed greens, cherry tomatoes, and a lemon vinaigrette can provide a refreshing contrast to the rich meatloaf. For a heartier accompaniment, garlic mashed potatoes or a creamy polenta can round out the meal.

Once the meatloaf is done, let it rest for a few minutes before slicing. This allows the juices to redistribute, ensuring each slice is moist and flavorful. As you cut into the meatloaf, you'll notice the pockets of melted feta, the vibrant flecks of sun-dried tomatoes, and the aromatic herbs, all coming together in a perfect bite.

One of the joys of making meatloaf is its potential for leftovers. Cold meatloaf makes an excellent sandwich filling, especially when paired with crisp lettuce, ripe tomato slices, and a smear of mustard or aioli on crusty bread. Alternatively, crumble leftover meatloaf into a skillet with some diced vegetables and eggs for a hearty breakfast hash.

For those looking to further customize their meatloaf, consider these additional twists. Incorporate shredded zucchini or carrots into the meat mixture for added moisture and a boost of vegetables. For a smoky barbecue version, mix in some chopped cooked bacon and use a barbecue sauce glaze. If you prefer a more decadent version, stuff the meatloaf with a center layer of cheese or sautéed mushrooms.

Meatloaf also lends itself well to different cooking methods. While baking is the most common, you can also cook meatloaf in a slow cooker for an ultra-moist texture. Simply shape the meat mixture and place it in the slow cooker, then cook on low for 6-8 hours. This method allows the flavors to meld together beautifully and keeps the meatloaf incredibly tender.

Roasted Chicken and Vegetables

Roasted chicken and vegetables is a timeless dish that epitomizes comfort and simplicity while delivering a burst of flavors and textures. Its beauty lies in the harmonious combination of juicy, tender chicken and caramelized, savory vegetables, all brought together by the magic of roasting. This dish is perfect for weeknight dinners or special gatherings, offering both ease of preparation and impressive results. Here, we'll delve into the nuances of creating the perfect roasted chicken and vegetables, from selecting ingredients to mastering roasting techniques.

Selecting the right chicken is the first step to a successful roast. Opt for a whole chicken that is free-range or organic, as these tend to have better flavor and texture. Ensure the chicken is patted dry with paper towels, both inside and out, which helps achieve a crispy, golden skin. Seasoning the chicken generously is crucial. A simple yet effective blend includes kosher salt, freshly ground black pepper, and a mix of dried herbs such as thyme, rosemary, and sage. Rubbing the seasoning all over the chicken, including under the skin and inside the cavity, ensures the flavors penetrate deeply.

For added flavor, consider stuffing the cavity with aromatics. A halved lemon, a few cloves of garlic, and sprigs of fresh herbs can infuse the chicken with subtle, fragrant notes as it roasts. Trussing the chicken, or tying the legs together with kitchen twine, promotes even cooking and helps maintain its shape.

Choosing the right vegetables to accompany your chicken is equally important. Root vegetables like carrots, parsnips, and potatoes are classic choices, as they roast well and develop a delicious caramelized exterior. Brussels sprouts, sweet potatoes, and red onions also make excellent additions, providing a variety of flavors and textures. Cut the vegetables into uniform pieces to ensure they cook evenly.

To prepare the vegetables, toss them in a bowl with olive oil, salt, pepper, and any additional seasonings you prefer. A sprinkle of garlic powder or a dash of smoked paprika can enhance the flavor profile. Arrange the seasoned vegetables in a single layer on the bottom of a large roasting pan or baking sheet. Placing the chicken on top of the vegetables allows the juices to drip down, flavoring them as they cook.

Roasting at the right temperature is key to achieving perfectly cooked chicken and vegetables. Preheat your oven to 425°F (220°C). This high temperature helps render the chicken fat and crisp the skin while ensuring the vegetables caramelize beautifully. Roast the chicken and vegetables for about 60-75 minutes, or until the internal temperature of the chicken reaches 165°F (74°C). Basting the chicken with its own juices halfway through cooking can enhance moisture and flavor.

An optional but highly recommended step is to start by roasting the chicken breast-side down for the first 20-30 minutes. This allows the juices to flow into the breast meat, keeping it moist. Afterward, flip the chicken breast-side up for the remainder of the cooking time to achieve that coveted crispy skin.

Resting the chicken after roasting is essential. Let the chicken rest for at least 15 minutes before carving. This resting period allows the juices to redistribute throughout the meat, resulting in a more succulent and flavorful chicken. Meanwhile, you can keep the vegetables warm by loosely covering them with aluminum foil.

Carving the chicken properly ensures each piece is as delicious as possible. Start by removing the legs and thighs, cutting through the joints. Slice the breasts against the grain to maintain tenderness. Arrange the carved chicken on a platter with the roasted vegetables around it, creating a visually appealing and appetizing presentation.

For an extra touch of flavor, consider making a simple pan sauce. After removing the chicken and vegetables from the roasting pan, place the pan on the stovetop over medium heat. Add a splash of white wine or chicken broth to deglaze, scraping up any browned bits stuck to the bottom. Let it simmer for a few minutes until slightly reduced, then swirl in a tablespoon of butter for richness. Drizzle this sauce over the carved chicken before serving.

While the classic combination of chicken and root vegetables is always a winner, don't be afraid to experiment with different flavors and ingredients. Mediterranean-inspired variations can include cherry tomatoes, bell peppers, and olives, seasoned with oregano and a squeeze of lemon. For a more exotic twist, try adding chunks of butternut squash, cauliflower florets, and a sprinkle of curry powder or harissa.

In addition to varying the vegetables, you can also play with different marinades for the chicken. A mixture of olive oil, lemon juice, garlic, and herbs creates a bright, zesty marinade, while a blend of soy sauce, honey, and ginger offers a sweet and savory Asian-inspired flavor. Marinate the chicken for at least a few hours, or overnight if possible, to allow the flavors to fully develop.

Roasted chicken and vegetables is a dish that lends itself well to meal prep and leftovers. The roasted vegetables can be repurposed into a hearty salad, tossed with some fresh greens and a light vinaigrette. Shredded leftover chicken can be used in sandwiches, wraps, or even added to soups and stews. The possibilities are endless, making this dish not only delicious but also versatile and practical.

For those mindful of dietary preferences or restrictions, this dish can easily be adapted. Use a variety of colorful vegetables to cater to vegetarian or vegan guests, roasting them with the same attention to seasoning and technique. For a gluten-free option, ensure all seasonings and marinades are free from gluten-containing ingredients.

Comforting Pasta Bakes

Few dishes evoke the sense of warmth and satisfaction quite like a comforting pasta bake. This beloved classic combines the rich, hearty flavors of pasta, sauce, and cheese, melded together into a bubbling, golden masterpiece. Whether you're looking for a quick weeknight meal or a show-stopping dish for a gathering, pasta bakes offer a versatile and crowd-pleasing option. Let's explore the art of creating the perfect pasta bake, from selecting ingredients to mastering cooking techniques.

Choosing the right pasta is the foundation of a successful pasta bake. Short, sturdy shapes like penne, rigatoni, or fusilli are ideal because they hold their shape well and trap sauce in their ridges and hollows. Cook your pasta just shy of al dente, as it will continue to cook in the oven, absorbing the flavors of the sauce without becoming mushy. Remember to salt your pasta water generously; this is your first opportunity to season the dish.

The sauce is the heart of a pasta bake, providing moisture and flavor. A classic choice is a rich tomato sauce, simmered with garlic, onions, and a blend of Italian herbs like basil, oregano, and thyme. For a meatier option, consider a hearty Bolognese sauce made with ground beef or sausage, slow-cooked to develop deep, robust flavors. If you're in the mood for something creamier, a béchamel or Alfredo sauce, enriched with cheese and a hint of nutmeg, offers a luxurious base.

Cheese is an essential ingredient in any pasta bake, contributing both flavor and texture. Mozzarella is a favorite for its meltability and mild, creamy taste. Combining it with sharper cheeses like Parmesan or Pecorino Romano can add depth and a pleasant, tangy contrast. For a more intense cheesy experience, consider using a blend that includes Gruyère or Fontina, which melt beautifully and add a nutty, rich complexity.

Incorporating vegetables into your pasta bake not only boosts its nutritional value but also adds layers of flavor and texture. Sautéed spinach, mushrooms, and bell peppers are classic additions that pair well with both tomato and cream-based sauces. For a more rustic touch, roasted vegetables like zucchini, eggplant, and cherry tomatoes bring a sweet, caramelized dimension. If you're aiming for a more seasonal approach, consider adding butternut squash or Brussels sprouts for a comforting fall or winter dish.

Protein options can elevate your pasta bake, transforming it from a side dish to a main course. Cooked chicken, whether grilled, roasted, or even from a rotisserie, can be shredded and mixed in for added heartiness. For a seafood twist, try using cooked shrimp or crabmeat, which pair wonderfully with creamy sauces. Vegetarian options like tofu or chickpeas can also be incorporated, providing protein while keeping the dish light.

Assembling your pasta bake is where the magic begins. Start by mixing your cooked pasta with the sauce and any additional ingredients like vegetables or proteins. Ensure everything is well-coated, as this prevents the pasta from drying out during baking. Transfer the mixture to a large baking dish, spreading it out evenly. Top generously with cheese, ensuring a good coverage that will melt and form a delectable crust.

Baking at the right temperature is crucial to achieving that perfect golden, bubbling top. Preheat your oven to 375°F (190°C). Bake the pasta uncovered for about 20-25 minutes, or until the cheese is melted and golden brown. If the top isn't browning as desired, you can switch to the broiler for the last few minutes, keeping a close eye to prevent burning.

Allowing your pasta bake to rest for a few minutes before serving is important. This resting period helps the dish set, making it easier to cut and serve while also allowing the flavors to meld further. Garnish with a sprinkle of fresh herbs like parsley or basil for a pop of color and an extra layer of freshness.

For those looking to prepare in advance, pasta bakes are wonderfully suited to meal prep. You can assemble the dish up to a day ahead and store it in the refrigerator, then bake it when you're ready. If freezing, it's best to do so before baking. Wrap the unbaked pasta bake tightly in plastic wrap and aluminum foil. When ready to enjoy, thaw it in the refrigerator overnight and bake as directed, adding a bit of extra time to ensure it's heated through.

Pasta bakes also lend themselves well to customization, allowing you to experiment with different ingredients and flavors. For a Mediterranean twist, consider using feta cheese, Kalamata olives, and sun-dried tomatoes, paired with a tomato-based sauce infused with oregano and thyme. For a taste of the American South, a Cajun-inspired pasta bake with andouille sausage, bell peppers, and a spicy cream sauce can be a delightful variation.

For those with dietary restrictions, pasta bakes can be easily adapted. Gluten-free pasta works well as a substitute, though you may need to adjust cooking times slightly. Dairy-free versions can be made using plant-based cheeses and cream alternatives, ensuring everyone can enjoy the comforting goodness of a pasta bake.

One of the joys of pasta bakes is their ability to bring people together. Whether it's a casual family dinner, a potluck with friends, or a special occasion, a pasta bake is a dish that invites sharing and savoring. The aroma that fills your kitchen as it bakes, the sight of the bubbling, golden cheese, and the first delicious bite all contribute to an experience that is both comforting and fulfilling.

For a complete meal, pair your pasta bake with a simple green salad dressed with a light vinaigrette, which provides a refreshing contrast to the richness of the pasta. Garlic bread or a crusty baguette can also be a wonderful accompaniment, perfect for sopping up any remaining sauce. A glass of wine, whether a robust red for a tomato-based bake or a crisp white for a creamier version, can elevate the dining experience further.

Shepherd's Pie

Shepherd's pie, a hearty and comforting dish rooted in British cuisine, has become a beloved staple in many households around the world. Traditionally made with minced lamb, vegetables, and a creamy mashed potato topping, this dish offers a perfect balance of flavors and textures. It's a versatile recipe that can be adapted to various dietary preferences and ingredients on hand, making it an ideal choice for both weeknight dinners and special occasions.

Choosing the right meat is the first step in crafting an authentic shepherd's pie. While lamb is the traditional choice, ground beef can be used for a variation known as cottage pie. For a leaner option, consider using ground turkey or chicken. If you're catering to vegetarians, lentils or a mixture of finely chopped mushrooms can provide a hearty, meat-like texture. Whatever protein you choose, ensure it is cooked thoroughly and seasoned well to form the flavorful base of your pie.

The foundation of shepherd's pie is the savory filling, which typically includes a combination of meat, onions, carrots, and peas. Start by sautéing finely chopped onions and carrots in a splash of olive oil until they begin to soften. Adding garlic for a few minutes enhances the aromatic base. Next, incorporate the ground meat, breaking it up with a spoon as it browns. Season generously with salt, pepper, and a touch of Worcestershire sauce to deepen the flavor. A tablespoon of tomato paste can add richness and a hint of sweetness to the mixture.

Once the meat is browned, it's time to create a luscious, thickened sauce to envelop the filling. Sprinkle a bit of flour over the meat and vegetables, stirring to coat evenly. Gradually pour in beef or chicken broth, stirring constantly to avoid lumps.

The sauce will thicken as it simmers, creating a cohesive filling. Adding a splash of red wine or stout can introduce a depth and complexity to the sauce, though this step is optional. Finally, stir in frozen peas, which will cook through in the oven, maintaining their bright color and texture.

The crowning glory of shepherd's pie is the creamy mashed potato topping. Choosing the right potatoes is essential; starchy varieties like Russet or Yukon Gold are ideal as they yield a fluffy, smooth mash. Peel and cut the potatoes into even pieces, then boil them in salted water until tender. Drain well and return them to the pot over low heat to evaporate any remaining moisture. This step ensures your mash isn't watery.

For a luxurious mash, add generous amounts of butter and warm milk or cream, mashing until smooth and creamy. Season with salt, pepper, and a pinch of nutmeg for a subtle warmth. For an extra touch of indulgence, fold in grated cheese like Cheddar or Parmesan. This not only enhances the flavor but also helps create a beautifully golden crust when baked.

Assembling the shepherd's pie is a straightforward yet satisfying process. Spread the meat filling evenly in a baking dish, ensuring an even distribution of vegetables and sauce. Spoon the mashed potatoes over the top, starting at the edges to create a seal that prevents the filling from bubbling over. Use the back of a spoon or a fork to create decorative swirls or ridges on the surface, which will crisp up nicely in the oven.

Baking at the right temperature is crucial to achieving a perfect shepherd's pie. Preheat your oven to 400°F (200°C) and bake for about 25-30 minutes, or until the top is golden brown and the filling is bubbling around the edges. If the top isn't browning to your liking, you can finish it under the broiler for a few minutes, but watch closely to prevent burning.

Allowing the pie to rest for a few minutes before serving is essential. This resting period helps the layers set, making it easier to slice and serve while ensuring each bite is filled with both filling and topping. Garnish with a sprinkle of fresh herbs like parsley or chives for a touch of color and freshness.

Shepherd's pie is an excellent candidate for meal prep and leftovers. It can be assembled ahead of time and stored in the refrigerator for up to a day before baking. If you plan to freeze the pie, it's best to do so before baking. Wrap the assembled pie tightly in plastic wrap and aluminum foil. When ready to enjoy, thaw it in the refrigerator overnight and bake as directed, adding a bit of extra time to ensure it's heated through.

Customizing shepherd's pie to suit different tastes and dietary needs is part of its charm. For a lighter version, consider using cauliflower mash instead of potatoes. Simply steam or boil cauliflower florets until tender, then blend with a bit of butter and milk until smooth. This low-carb alternative provides a similar creamy texture with fewer calories.

For those adhering to a vegan diet, shepherd's pie can be easily adapted. Use lentils or a plant-based ground meat substitute for the filling, and replace the Worcestershire sauce with a vegan alternative. For the mashed topping, use a non-dairy milk like almond or oat, and vegan butter. Nutritional yeast can add a cheesy flavor without the need for dairy.

Exploring international variations can also breathe new life into this classic dish. In France, a similar dish called hachis Parmentier layers mashed potatoes over a mixture of ground meat and vegetables, often including a hint of garlic and thyme. In Greece, moussaka features layers of eggplant, ground meat, and béchamel sauce, offering a Mediterranean twist. Embracing these variations can inspire you to experiment with flavors and ingredients, making the dish your own.

Serving shepherd's pie with complementary sides can enhance the meal further. A simple green salad with a light vinaigrette provides a refreshing contrast to the rich pie. Steamed green beans or roasted Brussels sprouts can add a healthy, vibrant touch to the plate. For a more indulgent option, consider serving with warm, crusty bread to soak up any remaining sauce.

The enduring appeal of shepherd's pie lies in its ability to bring comfort and satisfaction to the table. Its versatility allows it to be tailored to various tastes and dietary needs, making it a dish that can be enjoyed by everyone. By mastering the basic techniques and embracing the opportunity to experiment with flavors, you can create a shepherd's pie that is both traditional and uniquely your own.

Slow Cooker Pot Roast

A slow cooker pot roast embodies the essence of comfort food, transforming a tough cut of meat into a tender, flavorful masterpiece with minimal effort. This dish, often associated with home-cooked Sunday dinners, offers a delightful combination of succulent beef, hearty vegetables, and rich gravy, all melding together over several hours of slow cooking. The magic of a slow cooker lies in its ability to cook food gently and evenly, making it perfect for creating a pot roast that is both tender and full of depth.

Selecting the right cut of meat is crucial for a successful pot roast. Chuck roast is the most popular choice due to its marbling and connective tissue, which break down beautifully during the long cooking process. This results in a moist, flavorful roast. Other suitable cuts include brisket and round roast, though they might require slightly different cooking times. When choosing your meat, look for a piece with good marbling and a uniform shape to ensure even cooking.

Before placing the meat in the slow cooker, it's essential to brown it. This step, while not strictly necessary, adds a significant depth of flavor to the final dish. Heat a large skillet over medium-high heat and add a bit of oil. Season the roast generously with salt and pepper, then sear it on all sides until a deep, golden crust forms. This process caramelizes the surface of the meat, enhancing its natural flavors and creating a rich base for the gravy.

Once the meat is browned, it's time to prepare the vegetables. Classic choices include onions, carrots, and potatoes, which not only complement the beef but also absorb the savory juices as they cook. Cut the vegetables into large chunks to ensure they hold up during the long cooking time. You can also add other root vegetables like parsnips, turnips, or sweet potatoes for additional flavor and variety. Place the vegetables in the bottom of the slow cooker, creating a bed for the roast.

Next, it's important to build a flavorful braising liquid. This liquid will infuse the meat and vegetables with taste as they cook. A combination of beef broth, red wine, and Worcestershire sauce provides a robust base, while tomato paste adds a touch of sweetness and depth. For added complexity, include aromatics such as garlic, bay leaves, and fresh herbs like rosemary and thyme. Pour the liquid over the roast and vegetables, ensuring everything is well-coated.

One of the key benefits of using a slow cooker is its ability to maintain a low, consistent temperature, which is ideal for breaking down tough cuts of meat. Set the slow cooker to low and cook the pot roast for 8 to 10 hours. If you're short on time, you can set it to high and cook for 4 to 6 hours, but the longer, slower cooking time is recommended for the best results. Resist the temptation to lift the lid frequently, as this releases heat and extends the cooking time.

As the pot roast cooks, the connective tissues in the meat break down, resulting in a tender, fork-tender roast. The vegetables become infused with the savory juices, and the braising liquid transforms into a rich, flavorful gravy. Once the cooking time is complete, carefully remove the roast and vegetables from the slow cooker and place them on a serving platter. Cover with foil to keep warm while you prepare the gravy.

To make the gravy, strain the cooking liquid into a saucepan, discarding the bay leaves and any large herb stems. Bring the liquid to a simmer over medium heat. To thicken the gravy, create a slurry by whisking together equal parts cornstarch and cold water. Gradually whisk the slurry into the simmering liquid until it reaches your desired consistency. Season with salt and pepper to taste. For an extra touch of richness, you can stir in a pat of butter or a splash of cream.

Serving the slow cooker pot roast is a moment of triumph. Slice the roast against the grain to ensure maximum tenderness, and arrange the slices on a platter alongside the vegetables. Spoon the gravy over the top, or serve it on the side for guests to help themselves. Garnish with fresh herbs for a pop of color and added freshness. Pair the pot roast with crusty bread or buttery dinner rolls to soak up the delicious gravy, and consider a simple green salad or steamed green beans to round out the meal.

Leftovers, if any, are a bonus. Pot roast often tastes even better the next day as the flavors continue to meld. Store any remaining meat, vegetables, and gravy in an airtight container in the refrigerator for up to four days. Reheat gently on the stovetop or in the microwave, adding a splash of broth if needed to keep everything moist. Leftover pot roast also makes a fantastic filling for sandwiches, tacos, or even a hearty pot roast hash for breakfast.

For a variation on the classic pot roast, consider incorporating different flavor profiles. A Mexican-inspired version might include ingredients like cumin, chili powder, and chipotle peppers in adobo sauce, served with tortillas and fresh salsa. An Italian twist could feature garlic, rosemary, and a splash of balsamic vinegar, paired with polenta or pasta. The possibilities are endless, allowing you to adapt the basic pot roast recipe to suit your tastes and culinary inspirations.

The slow cooker pot roast is more than just a meal; it's a tradition that brings people together. The aroma that fills your home as it cooks, the anticipation of a hearty, comforting dinner, and the satisfaction of sharing a delicious meal with loved ones all contribute to its enduring appeal. With a bit of preparation and the gentle, hands-off cooking method of the slow cooker, you can create a pot roast that embodies the warmth and comfort of home-cooked food.

Chapter 5

Comforting Side Dishes

Creamy Mashed Potatoes

Creamy mashed potatoes are the epitome of comfort food, a staple side dish that complements a wide variety of meals. The secret to perfect mashed potatoes lies in selecting the right type of potato, using proper cooking techniques, and incorporating just the right amount of butter, cream, and seasoning. This classic dish, when done right, can elevate any dinner to new heights of satisfaction and indulgence.

Selecting the right potatoes is the first crucial step. Russet potatoes, with their high starch content, are ideal for achieving a fluffy, creamy texture. Yukon Golds, on the other hand, offer a naturally buttery flavor and a slightly denser consistency. Some cooks prefer a blend of both to balance fluffiness and flavor. Regardless of your choice, ensure the potatoes are firm and free of blemishes.

Start by peeling the potatoes. While some prefer leaving the skins on for added texture and nutrients, classic creamy mashed potatoes call for a smooth, velvety finish, which is best achieved with peeled potatoes. Cut them into uniform chunks to ensure even cooking. Typically, 1- to 2-inch pieces work well. This step is crucial as uneven pieces can lead to some parts being overcooked while others remain underdone.

Place the potato chunks in a large pot and cover them with cold water. Adding the potatoes to cold water and then bringing it to a boil helps them cook more evenly. Add a generous amount of salt to the water—this is your first layer of seasoning and ensures the potatoes are flavorful throughout. Bring the water to a boil over high heat, then reduce to a simmer. Cook the potatoes until they are fork-tender, which usually takes about 15-20 minutes.

While the potatoes are cooking, prepare your dairy mixture. The combination of butter and cream is what gives mashed potatoes their signature richness. In a small saucepan, gently heat the butter and cream together until the butter is melted and the mixture is warm. This step ensures that the dairy blends smoothly into the potatoes, preventing them from becoming gluey.

Once the potatoes are tender, drain them thoroughly and return them to the pot. Allowing the potatoes to sit in the hot pot for a few minutes helps to evaporate any excess moisture, resulting in a better texture. Now comes the mashing. For the creamiest results, a potato ricer or food mill is your best bet. These tools produce a fine, even mash without overworking the potatoes. If you don't have these tools, a traditional potato masher will also work, but avoid using a food processor or blender as they can make the potatoes gummy.

Gradually add the warm butter and cream mixture to the potatoes, stirring gently to combine. It's important to add the liquid slowly to avoid making the potatoes too runny. Season with salt and freshly ground black pepper to taste. For an extra touch of indulgence, you can add a dollop of sour cream or a handful of grated Parmesan cheese. These additions enhance the flavor and richness of the mashed potatoes.

Achieving the perfect consistency is a matter of personal preference. Some people love their mashed potatoes thick and hearty, while others prefer them light and airy. If you find the potatoes too thick, add a little more warm cream until you reach your desired consistency. Conversely, if they are too thin, you can let them sit for a few minutes to thicken up or add a bit more mashed potato to the mixture.

Once your mashed potatoes are smooth and creamy, it's time to serve. Transfer them to a warm serving dish and top with an extra pat of butter or a sprinkle of fresh herbs like chives or parsley for a pop of color and flavor. These simple garnishes can elevate the presentation and add a fresh element to the dish.

Leftover mashed potatoes can be a delightful treat. Store them in an airtight container in the refrigerator for up to four days. When reheating, add a splash of cream or milk to restore their creamy texture. You can reheat them gently on the stovetop over low heat, stirring occasionally, or in the microwave, stirring every minute to ensure even heating.

For those looking to experiment, there are numerous variations to explore. Adding roasted garlic or caramelized onions can impart a sweet, savory depth to the potatoes. Fresh herbs like rosemary, thyme, or dill can infuse the dish with aromatic complexity. For a tangy twist, consider mixing in some cream cheese or Greek yogurt. These variations can breathe new life into a classic dish and cater to different tastes and occasions.

Another creative approach is to incorporate different types of root vegetables. Mixing in parsnips, turnips, or sweet potatoes can add unique flavors and colors, making the dish more visually appealing and nutritionally diverse. These root vegetables should be cooked and mashed along with the potatoes, allowing their flavors to meld seamlessly.

For a healthier alternative, consider using cauliflower in place of some or all of the potatoes. Cauliflower mash is lower in carbs and calories but still offers a creamy texture and mild flavor. Steam the cauliflower until tender, then mash it using the same method as for potatoes, incorporating butter and cream to achieve the desired consistency.

When preparing mashed potatoes for a large gathering, you can make them ahead of time. Prepare the potatoes as usual, then transfer them to a slow cooker on the "keep warm" setting. This method keeps the potatoes warm and creamy for several hours, making them perfect for holiday meals or potlucks. Just give them a good stir before serving to ensure even consistency.

Mashed potatoes can also serve as a base for other dishes. Shepherd's pie, for example, features a layer of creamy mashed potatoes spread over a savory meat and vegetable filling, then baked until golden and bubbly. This dish transforms simple mashed potatoes into a hearty and satisfying main course. Another idea is to use leftover mashed potatoes to make potato pancakes or croquettes, adding a crispy exterior to the creamy interior.

Cheesy Mac and Cheese

Cheesy mac and cheese is the ultimate comfort food, beloved by both children and adults alike. Its creamy, cheesy goodness can turn any meal into a celebration. Perfecting this classic dish requires attention to detail, from selecting the right pasta to creating a smooth, flavorful cheese sauce. With a few tips and techniques, you can elevate your homemade mac and cheese to gourmet levels.

Choosing the right pasta is the first step. Elbow macaroni is traditional, but other shapes like cavatappi, shells, or penne can also work well. The key is to choose a pasta with plenty of nooks and crannies to hold onto the cheese sauce. Cook the pasta in a large pot of salted boiling water until just al dente. It should still have a bit of bite to it, as it will continue to cook when mixed with the hot cheese sauce. Drain the pasta and set it aside while you prepare the sauce.

The foundation of any great mac and cheese is the cheese sauce. A béchamel sauce, which is one of the classic French mother sauces, serves as the base. Start by making a roux, which is a mixture of fat and flour used to thicken sauces. Melt butter in a large saucepan over medium heat. Once the butter is melted and bubbling, add an equal amount of flour. Stir constantly to combine the butter and flour, cooking it for about 2-3 minutes until it forms a smooth paste and takes on a slightly golden color. This step ensures that the flour is cooked and will not leave a raw taste in the sauce.

Gradually whisk in milk, continuing to stir until the mixture is smooth and thickened. It's important to add the milk slowly to avoid lumps. Once all the milk is incorporated, bring the mixture to a gentle simmer. This is your béchamel sauce. To transform it into a cheese sauce, you'll need to add cheese. The type of cheese you choose can greatly influence the flavor and texture of your mac and cheese.

A combination of cheeses usually yields the best results. Sharp cheddar is a classic choice for its bold flavor and good melting properties. Gruyère adds a nutty depth, while mozzarella brings a creamy stretchiness. For a more complex flavor, consider adding Parmesan or even blue cheese in small amounts. Grate the cheese before adding it to the sauce to ensure it melts quickly and evenly. Stir the cheese into the béchamel sauce a handful at a time, allowing each addition to melt completely before adding more. Season the sauce with salt, pepper, and a pinch of nutmeg for a subtle warmth.

Once the cheese sauce is smooth and velvety, combine it with the cooked pasta. Ensure the pasta is evenly coated with the sauce. At this stage, you can serve the mac and cheese as is, but baking it adds a delightful golden crust. Pour the mac and cheese into a buttered baking dish. For an extra layer of flavor and texture, top it with a mixture of breadcrumbs and grated Parmesan cheese. Drizzle with a little melted butter to help the topping brown.

Bake the mac and cheese in a preheated oven at 350°F (175°C) for about 20-25 minutes, or until the top is golden and the sauce is bubbling around the edges. Let it rest for a few minutes before serving to allow the sauce to set slightly.

For those looking to experiment, mac and cheese is a versatile canvas. Adding mix-ins can turn it into a more substantial meal. Cooked bacon or pancetta adds a smoky, savory element. Steamed broccoli or peas introduce a pop of color and a bit of nutrition. For a gourmet twist, consider mixing in lobster or truffle oil. Whatever additions you choose, ensure they are cooked and ready to eat before mixing them into the mac and cheese.

Another way to elevate your mac and cheese is by experimenting with different cheeses. Fontina, havarti, and gouda are all excellent choices that melt well and offer unique flavors. Smoked cheeses can introduce a new dimension, while a touch of cream cheese can make the sauce even creamier. Be mindful of the balance, though; too much of a strongly flavored cheese can overpower the dish.

For a lighter version, you can substitute some of the milk with chicken or vegetable broth. Greek yogurt or cottage cheese can replace some of the traditional cheese, adding protein and a tangy flavor. Using whole wheat pasta or adding more vegetables can also make the dish more nutritious without sacrificing taste.

Leftover mac and cheese can be just as delightful as the fresh dish. Store it in an airtight container in the refrigerator for up to four days. Reheat it gently on the stove or in the microwave, adding a splash of milk or cream to restore its creamy consistency. You can also transform leftovers into mac and cheese bites by shaping the cold mac and cheese into balls, breading them, and frying them until golden and crispy.

For those who enjoy a bit of heat, spices can add an exciting twist to traditional mac and cheese. A dash of hot sauce or cayenne pepper can give it a subtle kick. Smoked paprika or ground mustard can enhance the flavor profile, making the dish more complex and interesting.

Mac and cheese holds a special place in many hearts, often associated with childhood memories and family gatherings. Its simplicity and versatility make it a dish that can be enjoyed in countless ways. Whether you stick to the classic recipe or venture into creative variations, the key is to use quality ingredients and pay attention to the details.

Perfecting your mac and cheese might take a bit of practice, but the effort is well worth it. Each step, from choosing the pasta to creating a luscious cheese sauce, contributes to the final dish. By experimenting with different cheeses, mix-ins, and seasonings, you can create a mac and cheese that is uniquely yours and sure to please any crowd.

Homemade Biscuits and Gravy

Fluffy, homemade biscuits paired with rich, savory gravy is a breakfast classic that evokes warmth and comfort. This dish, deeply rooted in Southern cuisine, transforms simple ingredients into something extraordinary. Crafting the perfect biscuits and gravy at home might seem daunting, but with a few tips and techniques, you'll be able to create a meal that rivals any diner or family kitchen.

The foundation of this dish is, of course, the biscuits. Homemade biscuits are tender, flaky, and buttery—a far cry from the dense, dry versions often found in stores. The key to great biscuits lies in the ingredients and the method. Start with high-quality all-purpose flour. Southern all-purpose flour, such as White Lily, is particularly light and perfect for biscuits. If you can't find it, any good-quality flour will do.

Cold, unsalted butter is essential. The colder the butter, the better the biscuits will be. This is because as the biscuits bake, the butter melts and creates steam, forming those desirable flaky layers. Cut the butter into small cubes and place them in the freezer for a few minutes before you begin mixing. Buttermilk is the traditional liquid used in Southern biscuits, providing a slight tang and extra tenderness. If you don't have buttermilk, you can make a substitute by adding a tablespoon of lemon juice or vinegar to a cup of milk and letting it sit for a few minutes.

To start, preheat your oven to 425°F (220°C) and line a baking sheet with parchment paper. In a large bowl, whisk together the flour, baking powder, baking soda, and salt. Add the chilled butter and use a pastry cutter or your fingertips to work it into the flour until the mixture resembles coarse crumbs. It's okay if some larger pieces of butter remain; these will help create the flaky layers. Make a well in the center of the mixture and pour in the cold buttermilk. Stir gently with a fork until the dough just comes together. Be careful not to overmix, as this will make the biscuits tough.

Turn the dough out onto a lightly floured surface and gently pat it into a rectangle about an inch thick. Fold the dough in half, then pat it out again. Repeat this process two or three times—this folding technique helps build layers. Finally, pat the dough out to about half an inch thick and use a floured biscuit cutter to cut out your biscuits. Press straight down without twisting to ensure the biscuits rise evenly. Place the biscuits close together on the prepared baking sheet; they will help each other rise higher. Brush the tops with a little melted butter or buttermilk, then bake for 12-15 minutes, or until golden brown. Transfer to a wire rack to cool slightly while you prepare the gravy.

Gravy is the soul of this dish, and a good sausage gravy should be rich, creamy, and packed with flavor. Start with fresh pork sausage; the kind you use will significantly impact the taste of the gravy. Breakfast sausage, whether mild or spicy, works well. In a large skillet, cook the sausage over medium heat, breaking it up with a spoon as it cooks. Once the sausage is browned and cooked through, remove it with a slotted spoon and set it aside, leaving the rendered fat in the skillet.

To make the roux, which will thicken the gravy, you need fat and flour. If your sausage was lean and didn't render much fat, you can add a little butter to the skillet. Sprinkle an equal amount of all-purpose flour over the fat and whisk constantly, cooking until the mixture is smooth and slightly browned. This usually takes about 2-3 minutes and helps eliminate the raw flour taste.

Slowly add milk to the roux, whisking continuously to prevent lumps. Whole milk is best for a rich, creamy gravy, but you can use any milk you prefer. Bring the mixture to a gentle simmer, stirring often until it thickens. This should take about 5-7 minutes. Return the cooked sausage to the skillet, stirring to combine. Season the gravy with plenty of freshly ground black pepper and a pinch of salt. If you like a little heat, a dash of hot sauce or a pinch of cayenne pepper can add a nice kick.

To serve, split open the warm biscuits and ladle the sausage gravy over the top. The biscuits should be tender and airy, soaking up the creamy gravy beautifully. This dish is best enjoyed immediately, but both components can be made ahead. The biscuits can be baked and stored in an airtight container for a day or two, and the gravy can be refrigerated and reheated gently on the stove, adding a splash of milk to loosen it up as needed.

For a twist on the traditional recipe, consider adding some cheese to the biscuit dough. Sharp cheddar or a mix of cheddar and Parmesan can add a deliciously savory note. Fresh herbs like chives or thyme can also be mixed into the dough for an added layer of flavor. Experimenting with different types of sausage, such as Italian or chorizo, can also bring new dimensions to the gravy.

While biscuits and gravy are often associated with breakfast, they make a hearty and comforting meal at any time of day. Pair them with scrambled eggs and fresh fruit for a balanced breakfast, or serve them alongside a simple green salad for a satisfying dinner. The leftovers, if there are any, can be transformed into a breakfast casserole by layering crumbled biscuits and gravy in a baking dish, topping with beaten eggs and cheese, and baking until set.

Warm and Buttered Cornbread

Cornbread, with its golden crust and tender crumb, holds a special place in many kitchens. Whether as a side dish to a steaming bowl of chili or a stand-alone treat slathered in butter and honey, cornbread's versatility and comfort are unmatched. Its roots run deep in American cuisine, particularly in Southern cooking, where it has been a staple for generations. Making warm and buttered cornbread from scratch is a simple yet rewarding process that transforms humble ingredients into a delightful culinary experience.

Begin with the basics: the ingredients. Cornmeal is, of course, the star of the show. Opt for a medium or fine grind for a smoother texture, though those who enjoy a bit of crunch might prefer a coarser grind. The type of cornmeal you use can influence the flavor and texture of your cornbread. Yellow cornmeal is traditional and imparts a sweet, corn-forward flavor, while white cornmeal offers a milder taste. Some recipes call for a mix of cornmeal and flour to achieve a balance of flavor and texture, ensuring the cornbread is neither too dense nor too crumbly.

Preheat your oven to 400°F (200°C) and, if you have one, place a cast-iron skillet inside to heat up. A hot skillet will give your cornbread a crispy, golden crust while keeping the interior moist and tender. If you don't have a cast-iron skillet, a regular baking dish will suffice, though you might not achieve the same level of crustiness.

In a large mixing bowl, whisk together the dry ingredients: cornmeal, flour, baking powder, baking soda, sugar, and salt. The amount of sugar can vary based on personal preference and regional traditions—some like their cornbread sweet, while others prefer it more savory. In another bowl, combine the wet ingredients: buttermilk, eggs, and melted butter. Buttermilk is essential for adding moisture and a slight tanginess, which enhances the overall flavor. If you don't have buttermilk, you can make a quick substitute by adding a tablespoon of vinegar or lemon juice to a cup of milk and letting it sit for a few minutes.

Make a well in the center of the dry ingredients and pour in the wet ingredients. Stir gently just until combined; overmixing can lead to tough cornbread. The batter should be thick and slightly lumpy. If you want to add a personal touch, this is the time to fold in extras like fresh corn kernels, diced jalapeños, shredded cheese, or chopped herbs. These additions can elevate your cornbread, making it unique and tailored to your taste.

Carefully remove the hot skillet from the oven and add a tablespoon of butter, swirling it around to coat the bottom and sides. This step not only prevents sticking but also contributes to that coveted crispy crust. Pour the batter into the skillet, spreading it out evenly. You should hear a satisfying sizzle as the batter hits the hot surface. This immediate contact with heat helps set the crust before the interior has a chance to rise and bake.

Bake the cornbread in the preheated oven for 20-25 minutes, or until the top is golden brown and a toothpick inserted into the center comes out clean. The edges should be crisp and slightly pulled away from the sides of the skillet. Let the cornbread cool in the skillet for a few minutes before slicing. This brief rest allows the interior to finish setting up and makes it easier to cut clean pieces.

Serving cornbread warm is ideal, as the butter melts into the crumb, creating a rich, indulgent bite. For a traditional approach, serve it with additional butter and honey on the side. The combination of sweet and savory is irresistible. Cornbread also pairs wonderfully with savory dishes like chili, barbecue, or hearty stews, where it can soak up the flavorful juices and add a contrasting texture.

For those looking to experiment, cornbread is a versatile canvas. Adding a handful of sharp cheddar cheese and a sprinkle of chopped chives to the batter can create a savory version perfect for pairing with soups. A touch of cinnamon and a handful of dried cranberries can transform it into a sweet treat ideal for breakfast or dessert. You can even use cornbread as a base for stuffing, combining it with sautéed vegetables, herbs, and broth for a delicious side dish during the holidays.

Cornbread is also an excellent way to use up leftover ingredients. Got some extra corn kernels from dinner? Toss them into the batter. Leftover cooked bacon can be crumbled and added for a smoky, savory twist. Even a dollop of sour cream or Greek yogurt can be mixed in to add moisture and a slight tang.

Storing leftover cornbread is simple. Wrap it tightly in plastic wrap or place it in an airtight container to keep it from drying out. It can be stored at room temperature for a day or two, but for longer storage, keep it in the refrigerator. Reheat slices in the oven or toaster oven to regain some of that fresh-baked warmth and crispness.

Cornbread's appeal lies in its simplicity and adaptability. It's a dish that can be dressed up or down, served at a casual family dinner or a festive holiday feast. Its roots in American culinary history add a touch of nostalgia and warmth, making it a beloved staple in many households. By mastering the basic recipe and experimenting with different flavors and additions, you can create a cornbread that's perfectly suited to your tastes and occasions.

Baked Sweet Potato Wedges

Baked sweet potato wedges are a delightful and nutritious alternative to regular potato fries, offering a unique blend of sweet and savory flavors. Perfect as a side dish or a snack, they are easy to prepare and can be seasoned to suit any palate. Their natural sweetness pairs beautifully with a variety of spices, making them a versatile addition to any meal. This chapter will guide you through the process of making perfectly baked sweet potato wedges, exploring techniques, seasoning options, and serving suggestions to elevate this humble vegetable into a culinary delight.

Begin by selecting your sweet potatoes. Look for firm, unblemished tubers with a deep orange hue, as these are often sweeter and more flavorful. Sweet potatoes come in different varieties, but for wedges, the orange-fleshed ones are ideal due to their moisture content and natural sweetness. Wash them thoroughly to remove any dirt, as the skin will be left on for added texture and nutrients.

Preheat your oven to 425°F (220°C) and line a baking sheet with parchment paper or lightly coat it with oil to prevent sticking. A high oven temperature is crucial for achieving a crispy exterior while keeping the inside tender.

To prepare the sweet potatoes, first, cut them into wedges. Slice the sweet potatoes in half lengthwise, then cut each half into quarters or sixths, depending on the size of the potato. Aim for uniform wedges to ensure even cooking. If some pieces are thicker than others, they may not cook at the same rate, resulting in unevenly baked wedges.

Once cut, soak the wedges in cold water for at least 30 minutes to remove excess starch. This step helps in achieving a crisper texture. After soaking, drain and pat the wedges dry with a clean kitchen towel or paper towels. Removing as much moisture as possible is key to getting crispy wedges.

In a large bowl, toss the sweet potato wedges with a couple of tablespoons of olive oil. The oil not only helps in crisping the wedges but also aids in the even distribution of the seasoning. Speaking of seasoning, this is where you can get creative. A simple combination of salt, pepper, and paprika is classic, offering a balance of savory and smoky flavors. For a spicier kick, add cayenne pepper or chili powder. If you prefer a hint of sweetness, cinnamon and a touch of brown sugar can complement the natural sugars in the sweet potatoes. Fresh or dried herbs like rosemary, thyme, or oregano can add an aromatic depth.

Spread the seasoned wedges in a single layer on the prepared baking sheet, ensuring they are not overcrowded. Overcrowding can cause the wedges to steam rather than bake, resulting in a soggy texture. If necessary, use two baking sheets or bake in batches.

Place the baking sheet in the preheated oven and bake for 25-30 minutes, flipping the wedges halfway through to ensure even cooking. The wedges are done when they are golden brown and crispy on the edges, with a tender interior. The exact baking time can vary based on the thickness of the wedges and your oven, so keep an eye on them to prevent burning.

While the sweet potato wedges are baking, consider preparing a dipping sauce to serve alongside them. A creamy garlic aioli, a tangy yogurt dip with fresh herbs, or even a spicy sriracha mayo can elevate the dish. These sauces can be made quickly and add an extra layer of flavor to the wedges.

Once the sweet potato wedges are done, remove them from the oven and let them cool for a few minutes on the baking sheet. This short cooling period allows them to crisp up further. Serve them warm with your chosen dipping sauce, and garnish with a sprinkle of sea salt or fresh herbs for a finishing touch.

Baked sweet potato wedges are not only delicious but also packed with nutrients. Sweet potatoes are rich in vitamins A and C, fiber, and antioxidants, making them a healthier choice compared to regular potatoes. Their vibrant color and sweet flavor can also make them more appealing to children and those who might be picky about vegetables.

For those looking to experiment further, sweet potato wedges can be adapted to various cuisines and flavor profiles. For a Mediterranean twist, toss the wedges with olive oil, garlic, and rosemary, and serve with a tzatziki sauce. For a touch of the

Caribbean, season with jerk spices and serve with a mango salsa. The possibilities are endless, and the adaptability of sweet potatoes makes them a favorite in many kitchens.

In addition to being a versatile side dish, baked sweet potato wedges can be a star ingredient in other recipes. Use them as a base for loaded sweet potato fries, topped with black beans, cheese, salsa, and avocado for a southwestern-style dish. They can also be added to salads, grain bowls, or even used in breakfast dishes alongside eggs and greens.

Storing leftover sweet potato wedges is simple. Allow them to cool completely before transferring to an airtight container. They can be stored in the refrigerator for up to four days. To reheat, spread the wedges on a baking sheet and warm them in a 400°F (200°C) oven for about 10 minutes, or until heated through and crispy again. Avoid microwaving, as this can make them soggy.

For those who meal prep, sweet potato wedges can be a great addition to your weekly routine. Prepare a batch at the beginning of the week and use them in various meals, from quick lunches to hearty dinners. Their versatility and ease of preparation make them a convenient and nutritious option.

Baked sweet potato wedges are a testament to how simple ingredients can be transformed into something extraordinary with just a little effort and creativity. Whether you're preparing them for a family dinner, a casual get-together, or as a healthy snack, they are sure to be a hit. Their balance of sweet and savory flavors, combined with a satisfying texture, makes them a beloved dish for many.